CATHOLIC UNIVERSITY OF AMERICA
CANON LAW STUDIES
NUMBER 49

EXCOMMUNICATION

ITS NATURE, HISTORICAL DEVELOPMENT AND EFFECTS

A DISSERTATION

Submitted to the Faculty of Canon Law of the Catholic University of America in partial fulfilment of the requirements for the Degree of

DOCTOR OF CANON LAW

by

FRANCIS EDWARD HYLAND, J. C. L.
Priest of the Archdiocese of Philadelphia

CATHOLIC UNIVERSITY OF AMERICA
WASHINGTON, D. C.
1928

Nihil Obstat:

✠ THOMAS J. SHAHAN, S. T. D., J. U. L.,
Censor Deputatus.

Washingtonii, D. C., die XV Maii, 1928.

Imprimatur:

✠ D. CARD. DOUGHERTY,
Archiepiscopus Philadelphiensis.

Philadelphiae, die XXII Maii, 1928.

TABLE OF CONTENTS.

PAGE

Foreword vii

PART I.

CHAPTER

I. Canon 2257. The Nature of the Censure of Excommunication 1

II. Historical Development of the Censure of Excommunication 11

I. Pre-Christian Excommunication 12

1. Pagan Analogies 12

2. Hebrew Excommunication 12

II. Christian Excommunication 14

1. The Right of the Church to Excommunicate .. 14

2. The Church has exercised this Right from the Beginning 16

3. Terminology 18

4. Mortal Excommunication 19

5. The Delivering to Satan 21

6. Anathema 22

7. Maranatha 25

8. Medicinal Excommunication 26

9. Medicinal Excommunication and Public Penance 27

10. The Denial of Episcopal Communion 30

11. Minor Excommunication 31

III. Canon 2258 and Canon 2267. *Vitandi* and *Tolerati*: Communication in Profane Matters 35

PART II.

THE EFFECTS OF EXCOMMUNICATION.

Preliminary Remarks 48

I. The Legislation of Canon 2232 48

II. The Distinction between a Declaratory and Condemnatory Sentence 50

CHAPTER

I. Canon 2259. Assistance at Divine Offices 53

II. Canon 2260 74

I. Reception of the Sacraments 74

II. Reception of the Sacramentals 78

III. Ecclesiastical Burial 83

III. Canon 2261 88

I. Active Use of the Sacraments and Sacramentals ... 88

II. Some Special Points Concerning the Sacrament of Matrimony 99

1. Assistance at Marriage 100

(A) Assistance at Marriage of Notorious Excommunicates 100

(B) Assistance at Marriage by Excommunicated Priests 103

2. Matrimonial Dispensations 106

(A) The *Vitandi* and the *Tolerati post sententiam* as the Confessor of Canon 1044 106

(B) The *Vitandi* and the *Tolerati post sententiam* as the Priest who assists at Marriage in virtue of Canon 1098, n. 2 107

IV. Canon 2262. Indulgences, Suffrages and Public Prayers: Application of Mass for Excommunicates 112

V. Canon 2263. 123
I. Legitimate Ecclesiastical Acts 123
II. Excommunicates as Plaintiffs in Ecclesiastical Courts 136
III. The Discharge of Ecclesiastical Offices 140
IV. The Use of Privileges 142

VI. Canon 2264. The Exercise of Jurisdiction 144

VII. Canon 2265 and Canon 2266 150
I. The Right of Election, Presentation, Nomination ... 151
II. Acquisition and Privation of Dignities, Offices, Benefices, Pensions, etc. 154
III. The Reception of Orders 157
IV. Pontifical Rescripts 160

VIII. The Indirect Effects of Excommunication 165
I. Irregularity 165
II. Suspicion of Heresy 166

Bibliography 168
Theses 177
Biographical Note 181

FOREWORD

The object of this present dissertation is to present, as briefly as the subject allows, a study of the nature, historical development and effects of the censure of excommunication. Excommunication is the gravest of all canonical punishments; it separates the delinquent from the communion of the faithful, and, practically speaking, deprives him of all the rights of membership in the Church of Christ. Were its dreadful character better known, no doubt the ends of ecclesiastical penal legislation would be more efficiently attained.

In the early ages the word *excommunication* was a generic term used to designate all ecclesiastical punishments and remedies. Consequently, the history of the censure of excommunication is very closely connected with that of ecclesiastical punishments in general; at times they are so closely allied that it is impossible to discriminate between them. Hence this work does not contain an exhaustive study of the history of excommunication. An attempt has been made, however, to gather together the salient points in its historical development.

Naturally, more attention has been given to the study of the effects of excommunication because of their practical importance. Excommunication is a medicinal punishment; its primary and immediate purpose is to bring the delinquent back to a sense of duty. The many and grave effects which follow upon the censure of excommunication are well calculated to accomplish this purpose. The effects of excommunication are, as Cerato (*Censurae Vigentes,* n. 37) remarks "totidem auxilia ac voces, quibus Pia Mater Ecclesia delinquentem et contumacem ad poenitentiam et ad salutem adducere contendit."

A few words must be added concerning the arrangement of the matter. The dissertation is divided into two parts. The first part comprises three chapters, which treat of the nature of excommunication, its historical development, the distinction between the *vitandi* and the *tolerati* and communication in profane matters. The last-mentioned subject should have been treated in the second part of the dissertation together with the other effects of excommunication. Since, however, it is so closely, in fact almost inseparably, united with the distinction between the *vitandi* and the *tolerati,* it was deemed more advisable to treat of it in connection with this distinction. The second part of the dissertation deals with the effects of the censure. In commenting upon the effects of excommunication, the writer has strictly adhered to the order of the canons.

The writer takes this occasion to express his sincere gratitude to the Faculty of Canon Law at the Catholic University for their kind interest and generous assistance throughout his course and especially in the preparation of this dissertation.

PART I

CHAPTER I

The Nature of the Censure of Excommunication

CANON 2257

§ 1. Excommunicatio est censura qua quis excluditur a communione fidelium cum effectibus qui in canonibus, qui sequuntur, enumerantur, quique separari nequeunt.

§ 2. Dicitur quoque anathema, praesertim si cum sollemnitatibus infligatur quae in Pontificali Romano describuntur.

Etymologically, excommunication (Lat. *ex,* out of, away from; *communicatio,* communication) signifies the separation of one from communication with others. In ecclesiastical law, it designates the act of excluding, or the state of being excluded from communication with the faithful, and is defined as a censure by which a person is excluded from the communion of the faithful with the effects which are enumerated in the canons and which cannot be separated.[1]

Generically, therefore, excommunication is a censure, that is, a penalty by which a baptized person, delinquent and contumacious, is deprived of some spiritual goods, or goods annexed to spiritual things, until he ceases to be contumacious and is absolved.[2] A censure is a penalty, that is, a privation of some good, inflicted by legitimate authority for the correction of the delinquent and punishment of the offence.[3] It is a spiritual pen-

1 Can. 2257, § 1.
2 Can. 2241, § 1.
3 Can. 2215.

alty, not only because it proceeds from a spiritual power and is inflicted for a spiritual purpose, but especially because it deprives one of spiritual goods, although secondarily it deprives one of temporal goods also.[4] Moreover, it is a medicinal penalty, for its primary and immediate purpose is the emendation of the delinquent.

In order that one may be punished by a censure, he must be baptized, delinquent and contumacious. He must be baptized, for only by a baptism does one become directly subject to the jurisdiction of the Church; baptism is a requisite for subjection to all ecclesiastical laws. He must be delinquent, that is, guilty of an external and morally imputable violation of a law or precept to which is added, at least indeterminately, a canonical sanction;[5] this is a requisite for incurring any ecclesiastical penalty. Finally, he must be contumacious; it is this element which is proper to censures and serves to distinguish them from all other ecclesiastical punishments; a censure is a medicinal penalty, its primary and immediate purpose being to correct the offender; hence it presupposes contumacy.

A censure deprives one of *some* spiritual goods, or goods annexed to spiritual matters. There are some spiritual goods of which the Church cannot by censure or any other means deprive the faithful, ex gr., divine grace, internal virtues, the power of orders, etc.[6] A censure can deprive one only of those spiritual goods which are within the power of the Church, ex. gr., the administration and reception of the sacraments, indulgences, jurisdiction, ecclesiastical burial, etc., and also of temporal goods which have some relation to spiritual matters, ex. gr., the emoluments of a benefice, the administration of ecclesiastical goods, etc.[7]

---

[4] Sole, *De Delictis et Poenis*, n. 157.
[5] Can. 2195.
[6] Sole, *De Delictis et Poenis*, n. 157.
[7] *Ibidem.*

Two conditions are required before a censure ceases; the contumacy must cease and absolution must be obtained.

Canon 2241, § 2 warns all who have the power to inflict censures to make a sober and careful use of them, especially of such as are incurred by the very commission of the delict (*latae sententiae*), and more particularly of excommunication. It may be well to repeat here the warning of the Council of Trent:

> Quamvis excommunicationis gladius nervus sit ecclesiasticae disciplinae et ad continendos in officio populos valde salutaris, sobrie tamen magnaque circumspectione exercendus est, cum experientia doceat, si temere aut levibus ex rebus incutiatur, magis contemni quam formidari, et perniciem potius parere quam salutem.[8]

There are three species of censures, namely; excommunication, suspension and interdict.[9] A brief comparison of them will not be amiss and will no doubt help to a better understanding of the nature and gravity of excommunication.

The interdict is a censure by which the faithful while remaining in communion with the Church are forbidden certain sacred benefits mentioned in the canons (2270-2277).[10] Suspension is a censure by which a cleric is forbidden the exercise of his office, or benefice, or both.[11]

Suspension, of course, can affect only clerics; an interdict, both clergy and laity. Both can be imposed upon a moral person, or community. An interdict can also be local. Excommunication can affect both clergy and laity, but only physical persons; hence if it is imposed upon a moral person or community, it is understood as affecting only the individuals who cooperated in the delict.[12]

---

8 Sess. XXV, *de Ref.*, cap. 3.
9 Can. 2255, § 1.
10 Can. 2268, § 1.
11 Can. 2278, § 1.
12 Can. 2255, § 2.

Interdict and suspension can be employed either as censures or as vindictive penalties. Excommunication, however, is always a censure; hence, it can never be inflicted for a determined period of time, but only until the guilty one has given up his contumacy and obtained absolution.[13]

Excommunication places one outside the communion of the faithful; interdict and suspension are punishments imposed upon persons while remaining in communion with the Church. The latter usually deprive a person only of some of the rights resulting from his position or membership in the Church; the former divests one of "all the rights resulting from the social status of the Christian as such."[14] The effects of excommunication concern personal spiritual benefits and favors, that is, such as touch the soul and salvation of the individual, whereas the privations entailed by the other two censures are not of such an individual spiritual character.[15]

Thus it is clear from what has been said, and it will be more apparent later on, that of the three species of censures, excommunication is by far the most severe. It is the gravest of all canonical punishments, "quum Ecclesia non habeat ultra quid faciat."[16] It is often likened to death. Saint Jerome[17] and Saint Augustine[18] compare it to the expulsion of Adam from Paradise. It is very aptly called *an exile from the Church of Christ.* "For as a Roman citizen condemned to exile lost all his rights of citizenship, so also does an excommunicate become divested of all his rights as a citizen of the city of God on earth, that is, as a member of the true Church."[19]

Specifically, excommunication differs from the other censures in this that it separates one from the communion

---

13 Can. 2255, § 2; cf. Can. 2241, § 1.
14 Boudinhon, "Excommunication," *Catholic Encyclopedia,* V. 678.
15 Cf. Suarez, *De Censuris,* disp. XVIII, s. 2, n. 3. Cf. however, can 2275.
16 C. 10, X, *de judiciis,* II, 1.
17 *Comment. in Osee,* lib. II, cap. IV, MPL, 25, 870.
18 *De Genesi ad Litteram,* lib. II, cap. XL, MPL, 34, 451.
19 Smith, *Elements of Ecclesiastical Law,* III, n. 3188.

of the faithful. What is to be understood by the *communion of the faithful?* It may be said that among the faithful there are three kinds of communion. In the first place, there is that purely internal communion by which the faithful are united among themselves and with Christ, and which consists in the bonds of divine grace, faith, hope and charity. Secondly, there is a communion among the faithful that is altogether exterior and comprises the ordinary civil and social relations of daily life. Finally, there is what might be called a *mixed* communion, consisting of "certain ecclesiastical and exterior acts and ceremonies that produce spiritual favors and blessings, by virtue of their institution, as the sacraments, the public prayers and suffrages of the Church, the Sacrifice of the Mass, benedictions and other religious ceremonies and public acts of divine worship: the satisfaction and merits of our Lord and the Blessed Virgin and the Saints, as contained in the treasury of the Church and dispensed by her to the faithful by means of indulgences." [20]

From which of these communions does excommunication exclude? It is clear that the Church cannot by excommunication or any other means deprive a person of that purely internal communion, consisting of divine grace and internal virtues. The existence of them does not depend exclusively on the will of the Church. They are not forfeited save by a voluntary action of the possessor. Sanctifying grace can be lost only by mortal sin. The infused theological virtue of charity is lost together with sanctifying grace by any mortal sin, but the infused theological virtues of faith and hope are forfeited only by the commission of mortal sins directly opposed to these virtues. Indeed, excommunication may be, and almost always is, a sign that sanctifying grace and one or more of the infused virtues have been forfeited. Of itself, however, excommunication does not and cannot destroy them. Moreover, it cannot prevent a per-

20 Smith, *Elements of Ecclesiastical Law,* III, n. 3190.

son from recovering sanctifying grace and the concomitant virtues, for one may do so by an act of perfect contrition.

Excommunication may divest one of that purely external communion consisting of the social and civil affairs of every-day life. Since communication in profane matters can and ought to be directed by the faithful to a spiritual end, and since the refusal of such communication is well calculated to bring the offender to repentance, there is no doubt but that the same can fall under the prohibition of the Church.

The communion of the faithful, however, from which excommunication primarily excludes is that which is called *mixed*, and which is composed of the faithful in so far as they constitute a society under the authority of the Church. By virtue of this communion, the faithful share in all the blessings of the Christian society which Christ wished to confer upon them through the ministry of His Church. By excommunication a person is deprived of participation in all such blessings. Hence an excommunicated person is not only excluded from legal ecclesiastical acts, forbidden the exercise of jurisdiction in both forums, deprived of the rights of election, presentation and nomination, etc., but is also deprived of such altogether spiritual blessings as the use of the sacraments, a participation in the indulgences, suffrages and public prayers of the Church, of the right to assist at the divine offices, etc., for all these Christ left to the administration of His Church. Thus we see how erroneous it would be to hold that the effects of excommunication are of a merely external character. Certainly a censure which deprived one of the right to assist at sacred rites, of a sharing in the indulgences, suffrages and public prayers of the Church, and, above all, of the use of the sacraments affects the very soul and prevents a man from acquiring countless and inestimable graces. In the Bull *"Exsurge Domine"* of June 15, 1520, Pope Leo X proscribed the following proposition (XXIII), formulated from the teachings of Martin Luther: "Excommunicationes sunt tantum externae poenae, nec privent hominem communibus spiritualibus Ecclesiae orationibus."[21] The forty-sixth proposition of the Synod of Pistoia asserting, "effectum excommunicationis exteriorem dumtaxat esse, quia tantummodo natura sua excludit ab exteriore communicatione Ecclesiae" was condemned in the Constitution "*Auctorem Fidei*" of August 28, 1794, "quasi excommunicatio non sit poena spiritualis, ligans in coelo, animas obligans."[22]

An excommunicate does not, of course, cease to be a Christian. The baptismal character is indelible and hence cannot be effaced by excommunication. Does such a one, however, cease to be a member of the Church? Since this question has more of a dogmatic than a canonical character, the writer will content himself for the most part with giving a résumé of the teaching of dogmatic theologians.

The question as to whether excommunicates cease to be members of the Church has given rise to quite a controversy among theologians.[23] Suarez is of the opinion that persons under ban of excommunication continue to be members of the Church. He states that the Fathers do not teach that excommunicates are placed outside the Church, but rather that they are separated from communication with the Church: that a person can retain his citizenship in a state and yet be deprived of the society of his fellow-citizens. "Quapropter excommunicatus non dicitur habendus ethnicus simpliciter, sed *tanquam ethnicus* quantum ad communicationem cum aliis."[24]

Bellarmine maintains that excommunicates cease to be members of the Church.[25] He argues in the first place from the text in Saint Matthew's Gospel: "If he will not hear the Church, let him be to thee as the heathen and publican."[26] He draws his second argument from a

21 *Fontes*, n. 76.
22 *Fontes*, n. 475.
23 Cf. Murray, *Tractatus de Ecclesia Christi*, disp. III, sect. VIII, n. 118.
24 *De Fide*, disp. IX, s. 1, n. 16.
25 *De Conciliis*, lib. III, cap. VI.
26 XVIII, 17.

canon in the Decree of Gratian which reads as follows: "Canonica instituta, et sanctorum Patrum exempla sequentes, Ecclesiarum Dei violatores, auctoritate Dei et judicio sancti Spiritus, a gremio sanctae matris Ecclesiae, et a consortio totius Christianitatis eliminamus."[27] He supports his contention by many references to the writings of the Fathers. His final argument is one of reason. In the first place, he points out that excommunicates are deprived of all spiritual communication which is common to the members of the Church; consequently, they are not members of the Church. Secondly, excommunication has the same place in the Church that the penalty of death had in the Old Testament and still has in civil society; but by death, men are entirely separated from society. Thirdly, excommunication is the most severe penalty which the Church can inflict; hence if excommunication does not deprive of membership in the Church, then there is a graver penalty than excommunication, namely, privation of membership in the Church. Fourthly, excommunication cannot be imposed except upon those who are contumacious; consequently it entails banishment from the Church; if excommunication was a penalty less severe than banishment from the Church, it would sometimes be imposed upon grievous sinners even though they were not contumacious. Finally, when excommunicates are absolved, it is said: "Restituo te unitati Ecclesiae et membrorum participationi";[28] this is an evident sign that the excommunicates were separated from the unity of the Church.

According to some of the more recent writers on dogmatic theology, the solution of the question hinges upon the will of the Church.[29] It is certain that the Church has the right and power to cut off entirely from membership in the Church not only heretics and schismatics, but like-

---

27 C. 107, C. XI, q. 3.

28 The latest edition of the Roman Ritual reads: " * * * restituo te communioni et unitati fidelium. * * * " Tit. III, cap. III.

29 Murray, *Tractatus de Ecclesia Christi*, disp. III, sect. VIII, n. 119; Mazzella, *De Religione et Ecclesia*, n. 609.

wise other grievous sinners.[30] Does the Church intend by excommunication to deprive one entirely of membership in the Church, or does she intend only to deprive the delinquent of the blessings and rights which accompany membership? In answer to this question, most of the recent dogmatic theologians distinguish between the *tolerati* and the *vitandi.* According to the more common opinion, the *tolerati* do not cease to be members of the Church, for the Church, in so far as she tolerates them, does not totally exclude them from her pale. With regard to the *vitandi,* the more commonly accepted opinion maintains that they cease to be members of the Church, since, at least temporarily, they are cut off from all external communion with the Church.[31] Tanquerey remarks that the question has little practical bearing, since the Church is wont to declare as *vitandi* only notorious heretics and schismatics who have already ceased to be members of the Church by reason of notorious heresy or schism.[32] Murray states that although it is not certain that the Church intends, *eo ipso et vi excommunicationis denuntiatae,* to expel every *vitandus* from the Church, the Church can pronounce excommunication in a form that will leave no room for doubt as to its intention.[33] A recent example of this was given by the Holy Office on November 8, 1922. In declaring two persons *vitandi,* the Holy Office stated that they were altogether expelled from the bosom of the Holy Church of God, "e gremio Sanctae Dei Ecclesiae penitus ejici." [34]

It must be remembered, of course, that all validly baptized persons can be said to be members of the Church, at least in the sense that *per se* they are subject to the laws of the Church. It would seem, too, that no notorious

---

30 Murray, *op. et loc. sit.;* Mazzella, *op. et loc. cit.;* Billot, *Tractatus de Ecclesia Christi,* p. 308.

31 Tanquerey, *Synopsis Theologiae Dogmaticae,* I, n. 905; Billot, *Tractatus de Ecclesia Christi,* p. 310; Mazzella, *De Religione et Ecclesia,* n. 608; cf. Murray, *Tractatus de Ecclesia Christi,* disp. III, sect. VIII, n. 119.

32 *Op. et loc. cit.*

33 *Op. et loc. cit.*

34 *AAS,* XIV, p. 593.

excommunicate retains full and perfect membership in the body of the Church, for such a one deprived, even in the external forum, of canonical communion which is one of the requisites for full and perfect membership in the body of the Church.[35]

Perhaps, after all, the foregoing controversy is one merely of words. Practically speaking, excommunicates are deprived of all the blessings and rights which accompany membership in the Church of Christ. Hence the question whether they are really deprived of membership in the Church seems to be one of theory and of little practical import.

Canon 2257, § 2 states that excommunication is also called *anathema,* especially when it is inflicted with the solemnities which are described in the Roman Pontifical. For an explanation of the term *anathema* and of its use in ecclesiastical penal legislation, the reader is referred to the chapter on the historical development of the censure of excommunication.[36]

---

35 Cf. Tanquerey, *Synopsis Theologiae Dogmaticae,* I, n. 897; Joyce, "Church," *Catholic Encyclopedia,* III, 755.

36 Chapter II, p. 22 ff.

CHAPTER II

Historical Development of the Censure of Excommunication

Excommunication, in general, is nothing more than the separation of one from the society of others. "Every human society which has an external organization must possess the right to expel from its body or membership any refractory member who, by his own fault, has rendered himself unworthy of belonging to it and enjoying its benefits and advantages. For it is plain that the expulsion of stubborn and ungovernable members is not only necessary to protect the honor and good name of a society, but, moreover, the only means of preserving its very existence. Hence we see, as a matter of fact, that every society, association, club or guild, no matter how small, has exercised and does exercise this power. Civil society or the State makes use of this power on a large scale. It cuts off bad and unruly citizens from communion with others by imprisonment, exile and even death." [1]

Religious societies are no exception to this rule. In fact, it is much more imperative that organizations whose principal aim is the sanctification of its members should have the right to expel from its communion obstinate members who, though repeatedly warned, nevertheless continue to scandalize others and bring religion itself into disrepute by their disgraceful living.[2] Thus it is that punishments analogous to excommunication were employed by the pagan and heathen religions of old.

---

1 Smith, *Elements of Ecclesiastical Law,* III, n. 3161.
2 Smith, *Elements of Ecclesiastical Law,* III, n. 3162.

I. Pre-Christian Excommunication

1. *Pagan Analogies*

Among the primitive Semitic peoples it was recognized that when persons were placed under a ban or taboo, restrictions were put on communicating with them and that the infraction of these was thought to involve supernatural dangers.[3] Among the Greeks there was the χερνιβῶν εἴργεσθαι,[4] that is, the exclusion of a person from purification with holy water. This penalty was incurred by persons guilty of bloodshed. The Roman *diris devotio* was a punishment somewhat similar to the Christian excommunication.[5] Caesar informs us that the inhabitants of Gaul who did not obey the decrees of the Druid priests were excluded from public worship and that among the Gauls this was a very grave punishment. Persons under ban of it were shunned by all.[6] Among the Germans, as Tacitus narrates, the greatest disgrace was incurred by losing a shield in battle. Persons guilty of this were deprived of all civil and religious rights. To many, death was preferable to such public contempt and to avoid it many hanged themselves.[7]

2. *Hebrew Excommunication*

The penalty of excommunication was in vogue among the Hebrews. In the first book of Esdras, we read that Esdras convoked at Jerusalem an assembly of all the Jews who had returned from captivity and decreed that "whosoever would not come within three days, according to the counsel of the princes and ancients, all his substance should be taken away, and he should be cast out of the company of them that were returned from captivity."[8] This was evidently excommunication, and there does not seem to be any sufficient reason for main-

---

[3] *Encyclopedia Brittanica*, Vol. X, art., "Excommunication."
[4] Demosthenes, 505, 14.
[5] Cf. Crnica, *Modificationes in Tractatu de Censuris*, p. 67.
[6] *De Bello Gallico*, lib. 6, c. 13.
[7] *Germania*, c. 6.
[8] X, 7ff.

taining, that before the time of Esdras, this sort of penalty was unknown.[9] It was a well-known penalty at the time of Christ who warned His disciples that they would have to suffer it for His sake.[10]

Hebrew excommunication consisted in the privation either of sacred or of civil rights, and sometimes of both.[11] Authors do not agree as to the number and kinds of excommunication which were in use among the Jews. Some mention three species, namely; Niddui, Cherem and Schammatha.[12] "The first marks the minor excommunication, the second the greater, and the third designates a still more terrible sort of excommunication to which the penalty of death is said to have been attached and from which no one could absolve." [13] It seems very doubtful, however, whether these three species of excommunication were in use among the pre-Christian Hebrews.[14] Selden maintains that there never existed among the Jews more than two kinds of excommunication, a greater and a lesser excommunication.[15] The former excluded a person for an indefinite period from the society of the members of the Hebrew Church; the latter excluded from social communication and from the synagogue, usually for a period of thirty days.[16] The discrepancy among authors as to Hebrew excommunication is, as Crnica remarks, "pro re nostra parvi momenti. Quod speciatim pro nobis valorem habet, est quod apud Judaeos excommunicationem jam in certa et determinata forma * * * extitisse tanquam medium omnino necessarium pro conservatione ordinis et disciplinae." [17]

---

9 Dixon, *A General Introduction to the Sacred Scripture*, II, p. 50ff; cf. Exodus XXX, 30, 38; XXXI, 14; Leviticus XVII, 4; Numbers XVI; Judges V, 23.

10 Dixon, *loc. cit.;* cf. Luke VI, 22; John IX, 22; XII, 42; XVI, 2.

11 Dixon, *op. cit.*, p. 51.

12 Cf. Smith's *Dictionary of the Bible*, I, art. "Excommunication"; Crnica, *Modificationes in Tractatu de Censuris*, p. 67; Dixon, p. 51.

13 Dixon, *loc. cit.*

14 Seisenberger, *Practical Handbook for the Study of the Bible*, p. 138.

15 *De Synedriis et Praefecturis Juridicis Veterum Ebraeorum*, L. 2, c. 7.

16 Dixon, *loc. sit.*

17 *Modificationes in Tractatu de Censuris*, p. 69.

II. Christian Excommunication

1. *The Right of the Church to Excommunicate*

The Christian Religion, too, has from the very beginning claimed and exercised the right to excommunicate gravely delinquent and contumacious members. There is no doubt but that the various kinds of excommunication employed by the Church in the early ages were somewhat similar to the Jewish forms of excommunication.[18] From this, however, we must not conclude that the excommunicatory discipline of the Church derived its origin from the Hebrew practice. The right of the Church to excommunicate is an immediate and necessary consequence of the fact that it was established by Jesus Christ as a perfect society for the salvation of souls. Consequently, the Church enjoys all the means which are necessary for the attainment of this end, and no doubt one of these means is the power of punishing delinquents, even, if necessary, by depriving them of communication with the Church.[19] This right which, as all admit, is necessary to every society that it may function well and survive, must with greater reason be acknowledged in the Church, whose principal object in punishing offenders with excommunication is to secure their emendation.

This argument from reason is confirmed by texts of the New Testament, the example of the Apostles and the practice of the Church throughout the ages. The words of Christ: "Whatsoever you shall bind upon earth, shall be bound also in heaven; and whatsoever you shall loose upon earth, shall be loosed also in heaven,"[20] refer not only to the power of forgiving sins but likewise to "all spiritual jurisdiction, including judicial and penal sanctions."[21] The words of Christ are general, "whatsoever you shall bind," "whatsoever you shall loose." Hence they include whatever may be necessary or even useful

---

18 Crnica, *Modificationes in Tractatu de Censuris,* p. 70.
19 *Ibidem.*
20 Matt. XVIII, 18.
21 Boudinhon, "Excommunication," *Catholic Encyclopedia,* V, 678.

for the proper government of the Church. Nor is there any reason for limiting the meaning of the words, which Christ Himself did not limit.[22]

Moreover, Christ explicitly granted to the Church the right to excommunicate. Speaking of an offender who remains contumacious even after being warned in the presence of two witnesses, Christ says: "And if he will not hear thee, tell the church. And if he will not hear the church, let him be to thee as the heathen and the publican."[23] The word *church* evidently has reference to the rulers and pastors of the Church. It is true that some have understood the word to mean the pastor together with the faithful among whom the offender resides. Indeed, in the primitive Church, scandalous sinners were sometimes denounced to all the faithful of the place, and if they remained obstinate, the bishop pronounced sentence of excommunication against them in the presence of the faithful.[24] Gradually, however, it came to pass that the sinner was denounced only to the bishop who alone, from the beginning, possessed the power to impose such penalties.[25]

There are four reasons which support the opinion that the word *church* in the above-mentioned text refers only to the pastors and prelates of the Church. In the first place, Christ ordered the Church to be heard, that is, obeyed: but such obedience is due only to the pastors of the Church. Secondly, the words which follow the text under discussion "whatsoever you shall bind," etc., most certainly refer only to the Apostles and their successors. Thirdly, although the method mentioned in the preceding paragraph was employed at times in the cases of scandalous and public sinners, the universal custom of the Church has always been to refer such matters to the legitimate ecclesiastical superiors. Finally, it would seem that Christ, in the text under consideration, had

22 Suarez, *De Censuris*, disp. I, s. 2, n. 3.
23 Matt. XVIII.
24 Ex. gr., I Cor. V.
25 MacEvilly, *An Exposition of the Gospels* (*Matthew & Mark*), p. 328.

reference to a private and occult crime, hence it would be against charity and a grave injustice to denounce the offender publicly.[26]

If the offender refused to obey the legitimate authorities of the Church, he was to be as the heathen and publican, that is, he was to be considered and treated as the Jews considered and treated the heathens and publicans. The Jews entirely refrained from communicating with the heathens and they regarded as infamous the publicans because of their injustice and oppression of the poor.[27]

2. *The Church Has Exercised this Right from the Beginning*

The right to excommunicate, inherent in the Church as in every properly constituted society, and explicitly granted to the Church by Christ Himself, was exercised from the very beginning of the Christian era. Saint Paul evidently excommunicated Hymeneus and Alexander, who had rejected faith and a good conscience,[28] and if he did not himself actually excommunicate the incestuous Corinthian, he judged the Corinthian to be worthy of excommunication and directed the Corinthian pastors "in the name of our Lord Jesus Christ" and "with the power of our Lord Jesus Christ to deliver such a one to Satan for the destruction of the flesh, that the spirit may be saved in the day of our Lord Jesus Christ."[29] In both cases, the Apostle speaks of delivering the delinquents to Satan. This is evidently effected by expelling them from the Church, for by being driven out of the Church, they "were placed in the kingdom of Satan since his is the other kingdom that is arrayed against the Church, the Kingdom of God."[30] "Omnis Christianus, dilect-

26 *The Great Commentary of Cornelius a Lapide,* translated by T. W. Mossman, St. Matthew, chap. X-XXI, pp. 303-305. MacEvilly, *An Exposition of the Gospels,* (*Matthew & Mark*), p. 328.

27 MacEvilly, *An Exposition of the Gospels,* (*Matthew & Mark*), p. 328.

28 I Tim. I, 20.

29 I Cor. V.

30 MacEvilly, *An Exposition of the Epistles of Saint Paul,* etc., Vol. II, p. 90.

issimi," writes Saint Augustine, "qui a sacerdotibus excommunicatur, satanae traditur: * * * quia extra ecclesiam est diabolus, sicut in ecclesia Christus, ac per hoc quasi diabolo traditur qui ab ecclesiastica communione removetur. Unde illos, quos tunc Apostolus satanae traditos predicat excommunicatos a se esse demonstrat."[31] It is to be noted that in both cases the object of the punishment is to secure the emendation of the offender: "that they may learn not to blaspheme"; "that the spirit may be saved in the day of our Lord Jesus Christ."

In the Epistles of Saint Paul there are references to the practice of regarding a person as anathema. Thus the Apostle invoked the anathema against those who love not our Lord Jesus Christ, and against anyone, angel or man, who preached a doctrine different from that which he preached.[32]

The faithful are frequently warned by the Apostles to avoid the company of sinful brethren.[33] Such warnings doubtlessly have reference to persons who, if not formally excommunicated, were practically at least regarded as such. If the faithful were not allowed to associate with them even in civil and profane affairs, may it reasonably be supposed that the Apostles placed no restrictions on the presence of such sinners at the Eucharistic sacrifice and the public assemblies of the faithful?

It is clear from the Epistles, therefore, that the penalty of excommunication was in use during the lifetime of the Apostles and that it was employed principally for corrective and protective rather than punitive purposes. In the pastoral Epistles,[34] it is apparent that even in the lifetime of the Apostles there was gradually developing a formal and recognized mode of proceeding in ecclesiastical disciplinary matters.[35]

---

31 C. 32, C. XI, q. 3.
32 I Cor. XVI, 17; Tit. III, 10; Rom. IX, 3.
33 Rom. XVI, 17; Tit. III, 10; I Cor. V. 9ff.; II John, 10-11.
34 I Tim. V. 19-20; Tit. III, 20.
35 *Encyclopedia Brittanica,* Vol. X, art., "Excommunication."

The example of the Apostles in this matter was followed by Popes, Councils and Bishops in all ages. The penalty of excommunication was inflicted not only on private individuals who were guilty of serious offenses and who refused obstinately to repent, but also on Emperors, Kings and Princes who were in like manner guilty.[36] It would be useless to consume time and space confirming this statement. It is proven from almost countless documents. What is more, it is practically admitted by all. What is of more importance is to determine how many species of excommunication have existed in the discipline of the Church. Before proceeding to this question, it might be well to say a few words concerning the terminology used by the Church in connection with this penalty.

3. *Terminology*

The penal terminology of the Church was, of course, a gradual development. It must not be supposed that total separation from the communion of the Church has always been expressed by the term *excommunication.* On the contrary, many and varied were the expressions used to designate this penalty,[37] ex. gr., *ab ecclesia haberi extraneus;*[38] *de ecclesiae communione pelli;*[39] *separare ab ecclesia;*[40] *a communione orationis et conventus et omnis sancti commercii relegari;*[41] *segregare ab ecclesiae corpore;*[42] *anathematizare;*[43] ἐκβαλλειν ἐκκλησίας[44]; ἀποβάλλεσθαι τῆς ἐκκλησίας.[45]

---

36 Cf. *Disputationes Marii Alterii, De Censuris Ecclesiasticis,* tom. I, lib. I, disp. III, cap. 3.
37 Cmica, *Modificationes in Tractatu de Censuris,* p. 71.
38 C. of Elvira (306) c. 41, Mansi 2, 12; C. of Agde (506) c. 42, Mansi 8, 332.
39 C. of Agde, (506) c. 8, Mansi 8, 332.
40 C. of Sargossa (691) c. 5, Mansi 3, 635.
41 Tertullian, *Apologetic.,* c. 39, MPL, 1, 469.
42 C. 32, D. 50; C. 2, C. XV, q. 5; C. of Lerida (524) c. 5, Mansi 8, 613.
43 C. of Sargossa, c. 1-4, Mansi 3, 634ss.; II C. of Carthage (390) c. 8, Mansi 3, 695.
44 C. of Sardica, (343) c. 14, Mansi 3, 17; c. 4, C. XI, q. 3.
45 Can. Apost., 51, 62.

On the other hand, it would be equally wrong always to understand the term *excommunicate* or *excommunication* as found in documents even as late as the twelfth century in the sense of total exclusion from the Christian community. At first *excommunication* was a generic term used to designate all ecclesiastical punishments and remedies. Thus it was employed sometimes to designate exclusion from the communion of the faithful, sometimes to signify merely the privation of some right or rights belonging to the faithful, or to a certain class among them. Then, as now, there were in the Church certain rights which were common to all the faithful, ex. gr., the reception of the sacraments, presence at Holy Mass and public prayers; there were other rights which were proper to the various grades among the clergy. Whoever, therefore, was deprived of all these rights, or of one or a number of them, might be designated by the general term *excommunicated*, that is, placed outside the communion to which his position in the Christian society entitled him.[46]

"When in the middle of the ninth century, the forum *externum* and the forum *sacramentale* had become more distinctly separated, the distinction was more clearly made also between penances and punishments which pertained to the external order. But for some time yet, the term excommunication continued to be applied to various kinds of punishments. It was only in the twelfth and thirteenth centuries that its technical meaning became definitely fixed, and the term employed to designate exclusively one of the three penalties which were thereafter distinguished from all others by the name of censures."[47]

4. *Mortal Excommunication*

In treating of the discipline of the early Church, authors usually make mention of two species of excommuni-

---

46 Berardi, *Commentarium in Jus Ecclesiasticum,* II, pt. II, diss. 3, cap. 5.
47 Ayrinhac, *Penal Legislation in the New Code,* p. 116.

cation, namely, mortal excommunication and medicinal excommunication.[48]

Mortal excommunication (*παντελὴς ἀφορισμός*, *omnimoda separatio*) was inflicted upon persons who were guilty of very serious offences and who refused contumaciously to repent. Persons under ban of this penalty were entirely deprived of communion with the Church, and hence were excluded not only from a participation in the Eucharist, but also from the prayers of the faithful and from hearing the Scriptures in any ecclesiastical assembly.[49] Four points may be mentioned concerning mortal excommunication.[50] 1) It was compared to the expulsion of Adam from Paradise.[51] 2) Usually when one fell under this censure, the neighboring churches, and sometimes all the churches of the Christian world, were notified by letter of the fact, that they might ratify the sentence and refuse to admit the excommunicate to their communion.[52] 3) A person excommunicated by one church was held to be excommunicated by all the churches: no other bishop or church could receive him.[53] Sometimes the same penalty was incurred by anyone who admitted an excommunicate to public or even private communion.[54] 4) All under ban of mortal excommunication were denied communication even in the civil and social affairs of daily life.[55]

Mortal excommunication has existed from the beginning of Christianity. Prescinding from the extraordinary effects which the *delivering to Satan* may have had in Apostolic times, it was undoubtedly this punishment which was imposed upon the incestuous Corinthian and

---

48 Devoti, *Lib. IV Institutionum Canonicarum*, tom. IV, tit. XVIII, § IV; Bingham, *Antiquities*, bk. XVI, ii, 8.

49 Devoti, *loc. cit.*

50 Bingham, *loc. cit.*

51 Cf. *supra*, p. 4.

52 Socrates, *Historia Ecclesiastica*, L. 1, c. 6, MPG, 67, 42, 43; Theodoret, *Historia Ecclesiastica*, L. 1, c. 4, MPG, 82, 910-911.

53 Can. Apost., 13, 32; C. of Nice (325) c. 5, Mansi 2, 670; C. of Sardica (343) c. 13, Mansi 3, 15.

54 Can. Apost., 13; II C. of Carthage (390) c, 7, Mansi 3, 694.

55 Cf. Chap. III.

upon Hymeneus and Alexander. Mortal excommunication and anathema were essentially the same penalty. Later mortal excommunication became known as major excommunication to distinguish it from minor excommunication, although long before the abolition of the latter, it was decreed that the word *excommunication* used without any modification was to designate major excommunication.[56]

5. *The Delivering to Satan*

Almost all commentators agree that the phrase *to deliver to Satan* designates at the very least the dread sentence of excommunication, especially when such a penalty is imposed nominally and publicly. Certainly one who is cut off from communion with the Church can be said to be delivered to Satan in this sense, that, deprived of so many means of grace, he is more exposed to and more easily conquered by the tyranny and incursions of Satan.[57] Again, such an expression may have reference to the corporal afflictions which one would have to endure by reason of being deprived of all communication, sacred and profane, with the faithful.[58]

Many commentators, however, are of the opinion that in Apostolic times the delivering to Satan implied much more than the spiritual punishment of excommunication. They maintain that persons thus punished were handed over to Satan in much the same way as Job, and consequently were subject to corporal vexations and torments inflicted by the evil one. This opinion has the support of Saint John Chrysostom[59] and of most of the Greek Fathers, and among the Latin Fathers of Saints Pacianus,[60] Ambrose[61] and Augustine.[62] Certainly corporal

56 C. 59, X, *de sententia excommunicationis*, V. 39.
57 Estius, *In Omnes Pauli Epistolas, itemque in Catholicas Commentarii*, II, 205.
58 MacEvilly, *An Exposition of the Epistles of St. Paul*, I, 174.
59 *Hom. 15, in I Cor.*, MPG 61, 123.
60 *Epis. 3 ad Sempr.*, MPL 13, 1075.
61 *De Poenitentia*, Lib. 1, c. 13, MPL 16, 484-485.
62 *De Sermone Domini in Monte*, lib. 1, c. 20, MPL 34, 1263.

afflictions and torments were effects of sin not uncommon in the early ages.

The ancient canons very seldom used the phrase under discussion. Saint Basil mentioned it once.[63] In the Decree of Gratian there is an epistle of Pope Pelagius which reads as follows: "Apostolicae auctoritatis exemplo didicimus, errantium et in errorem mittentium spiritus tradendos esse Satanae, ut blasphemare dediscant."[64] The phrase in these passages, however, seems to imply no more than the spiritual delivering over to Satan, that is, expulsion from communion with the Church, or excommunication, without any reference to bodily afflictions.

6. *Anathema*

Anathema (from Gr. ἀνάθεμα or ἀνάθημα: Lat. *anathĕma* or *anathēma*) literally signifies "set apart," "placed on high." The classical Greek form ἀνάθημα (Lat. *anathēma*) was the technical term used to designate a gift or offering made to a god in reparation for an offence, in thanksgiving for a favor, or with a view to propitiation.[65] Usually such gifts or offerings were suspended from the walls of the temple that they might be seen by all. "As odious objects were also exposed to view, e. g., the head of a criminal or of an enemy, or his arms or spoils, the word *anathema* came to signify a thing hated or execrable, devoted to public abhorrence or destruction."[66]

In the form ἀνάθεμα (Lat. *anathĕma*), the word is employed in Sacred Scripture as the equivalent of the Hebrew *herem.* "To understand the word anathema," says Vigouroux, "we should first go back to the real meaning of *herem,* of which it is the equivalent. *Herem* comes from the word *haram,* to cut off, to separate, to curse, and indicates that which is cursed and condemned to be cut off or exterminated, whether a person or a

63 *Epis. CLXXXIII,* c. 7, MPG 32, 675.
64 C. 13, C. XXIV, q. 3.
65 *Encyclopedia Brittanica,* Vol. I, art., "Anathema."
66 Gignac, "Anathema," *Catholic Encyclopedia,* I, 455.

thing, and consequently that which man is forbidden to make use of."[67] In Arabic the root h-r-m signifies simply "to set apart," "to separate." Hence the idea of destruction is a secondary meaning of the word which gradually lost its primitive signification of gift, offering.[68] However, the word occurs a few times in Sacred Scripture in its primary sense.[69]

In the Old Testament, "nations, individuals, animals and inanimate objects may become anathema, i. e., cursed and devoted to destruction. * * * When a people was anathematized by the Lord, they were to be entirely exterminated. Saul was rejected by God for having spared Agag, King of the Amalecites, and the greater portion of the booty (I K. xv, 9-23). Anyone who spared anything belonging to a man who had been declared anathema, became himself anathema. * * * Sometimes it is cities that are anathematized. When the anathema is rigorous all the inhabitants are to be exterminated, the city burned, and permission denied ever to rebuild it, and its riches offered to Jehovah. This was the fate of Jericho (Jos., vi, 17). If it is less strict, all the inhabitants are to be put to death, but the herds may be divided among the victors (Jos., viii, 27). The obligation of killing all inhabitants occasionally admits of exceptions in the case of young girls who remain captives in the hands of the conquerors (Num., xxxi, 18). The severity of the anathema in the Old Testament is explained by the necessity there was of preserving the Jewish people and protecting them against the idolatry professed by the neighbouring pagans."[70]

In the New Testament, anathema designates separation from God, or from the society of the faithful.[71] But he who is separated from God is cursed, hence the word is also employed as a malediction.[72] At an early date,

67 *Dictionnaire de la Bible* I, 545, (translated in *Cath. Ency.*, I, 455).
68 *Encyclopedia Brittanica,* Vol. 1, art., "Anathema."
69 Judith XVI, 23; II Mach. IX, 16; Luke XXI, 15.
70 Gignac, "Anathema," *Catholic Encyclopedia,* I, 455.
71 Rom. IX, 3; Gal. I, 9.
72 I. Cor. XVI, 22.

the Church adopted the word into its penal terminology to signify the total exclusion of one from the Christian community. Generally, however, it was employed to designate the excommunication incurred for heresy. All the councils from Nice to that of the Vatican have worded their dogmatic canons: "If any one say * * * let him be anathema." [73]

At first the anathema, as pronounced against persons, did not differ from the sentence of excommunication. It would seem, however, that a distinction arose between them sometime in the sixth century and continued until the time of Pope Gregory IX. Thus a canon of the Council of Tours speaks of a usurper of church goods dying "not only excommunicated, but anathematized." [74] In the Decree of Gratian we read: "Know that Engeltrude is not only under ban of excommunication, which separates her from the society of the brethren, but under the anathema which separates from the body of Christ, which is the Church." [75] Most canonists seem to be of the opinion that there was never an essential distinction between anathema and excommunication. They attribute the seeming difference between them during the period mentioned above to the fact that before the time of Gregory IX, the word *anathema,* when used in opposition to *excommunication,* designated major excommunication, while the term *excommunication,* used in opposition to *anathema,* signified minor excommunication.[76] Since Gregory IX declared that the term *excommunication,* used without any modification, was to be understood as major excommunication,[77] there has been no difference between the latter and anathema, except a greater or less solemnity in pronouncing the sentence.[78] It is this distinction which is recognized and retained by the Code,

---

73 Gignac, "Anathema," *Catholic Encyclopedia,* I, 456.
74 Can. 24, Mansi 9, 803-804.
75 C. 13, C. III, q. 4 (translated in the *Catholic Encyclopedia,* I, 456).
76 Cf. Suarez, *De Censuris,* disp. VIII, s. 2, n. 4-9; Wernz, VI, n. 179; Augustine, *Commentary,* VIII, p. 169.
77 C. 59, X, *de sententia excommunicationis,* V. 39.
78 Gignac, "Anathema," *Catholic Encyclopedia,* I. 456.

which informs us that excommunication is likewise called anathema, especially when it is inflicted with the solemnities described in the Roman Pontifical.[79]

7. *Maranatha*

In the first Epistle to the Corinthians, Saint Paul writes: "If any man love not our Lord Jesus Christ, let him be anathema, maranatha."[80] There has been quite a discussion as to the proper signification of the word *maranatha.*[81] Saint John Chrysostom says that it is a Hebrew word, signifying "*Dominus noster venit.*" He uses it to reprove those who continue in sin despite the fact that the Lord had come among them.[82] Saint Jerome understands the word in the same sense, although he claims that it is more a Syriac than a Hebrew term. He employs it against those who denied that the Lord had come among them.[83] Understood in this sense, maranatha added nothing to the penalty of excommunication, but was only a reason for pronouncing such a sentence against those who denied the coming of Christ either in word, as the Jew, or by disgraceful lives, as in the case of bad Christians.[84] Saint Augustine asserts that maranatha is a Syriac word, signifying "*Donec Dominus redeat.*"[85]

Whatever the meaning of the word, it was hardly ever used in any ancient form of excommunication. In the few places in which it does occur,[86] it seems to signify "in the coming of the Lord" or "until the coming of the Lord."[87] Maranatha did not add another punishment to that of excommunication, but merely increased its ex-

---

79 Can. 2257, § 2.
80 I Cor. XVI, 22.
81 *Devoti, Lib. IV Institutionum Canonicarum,* tom. II, tit XVIII, tit. § VII, not. 3.
82 *Hom. 44 in I Cor.* n. 3, MPG 61, 377.
83 *Epis. 26 ad Marcellam,* n. 4, MPL 22, 431.
84 Bingham, *Antiquities,* bk. XVI, ii, 16.
85 *Epis.* 20, n. 15.
86 III C. of Toledo, (589) c. 18, Mansi 9, 986; IV C. of Toledo, (633) c. 74, Mansi 10, 639.
87 *Encyclopédie de La Théologie Catholique,* "Maranatha," XIV, 201.

ternal solemnity. It is not to be understood as rigorously as some have thought, as though it absolutely separated one from the Church without any hope of reconciliation. Such an opinion is certainly most false, as it is opposed to the end of the Church and the divine economy of Redemption.[88] The "anathema maranatha is a censure from which the criminal may be absolved; although he is delivered to Satan and his angels, the Church, in virtue of the Power of the Keys, can receive him once more into the communion of the faithful. More than this, it is with this purpose in view that she takes such rigorous measures against him, in order that by the mortification of his body, his soul may be saved on the last day. The Church, animated by the spirit of God, does not wish the death of the sinner, but rather that he be converted and live. This explains why the most severe and terrifying formulas of excommunication, containing all the rigors of the maranatha have, as a rule, clauses like this: Unless he becomes repentent, or gives satisfaction, or is corrected." [89]

8. *Medicinal Excommunication*

Medicinal excommunication (ἀφορισμός, *separatio*) was inflicted upon those who were guilty of offences of a less serious character and also upon persons who had committed very grave offences but who acknowledged their sins and sought from the Church penance and peace. There seems to have been two grades to this lesser excommunication. Some who were under ban of it were deprived only of a participation in the Eucharist, while others, in addition to this, were excluded from the prayers of the faithful and had to pray with the catechumens.[90] Theodoret, when speaking of those who had sinned rather through weakness than malice, says that they should be excluded from the holy mysteries, but not

88 Cappello, *De Censuris*, n. 140.

89 Gignac, "Anathema," *Catholic Encyclopedia*, I, 456.

90 Devoti, *Lib. IV Institutionum Canonicarum*, tom. IV, tit. XVIII, § IV; Bingham, *Antiquities*, bk. XVI, ii. 7.

from the prayers of the catechumens. "Arceantur, inquit, a participatione sacrorum mysteriorum, a catechumenorum autem oratione non prohibeantur, neque divinarum scripturarum auditione, neque a magistrorum auditione." [91] A canon of Gregory Thaumaturgus speaks of an excommunication from prayers, which most likely has reference to the prayers of the faithful, and not the prayers of the catechumens, at which excommunicates might assist despite their exclusion from the other.[92] The Council of Lerida decreed that those who were guilty of certain sins of impurity should be admitted to the church only for the Mass of the catechumens.[93]

That there was even a lesser degree of excommunication, which excluded one from participation in the Eucharist, seems clear from one of the canons of the Council of Elvira, which reads as follows: "Virgines quae virginitatem suam non custodierint, si eosdem, qui eas violaverint, duxerint et tenuerint (maritos), eo quod solas nuptias violaverint, post annum sine poenitentia reconciliari debebunt." [94] The phrase "post annum sine poenitentia reconciliari debebunt" must not be understood in the sense that they were not obliged to receive the Sacrament of Penance, but in the sense that they were not obliged to pass through the various stages of public penance. Hence it would seem that their punishment consisted solely in the privation of the Eucharist.[95] A similar punishment for trigamists is mentioned in the canons of Saint Basil.[96]

9. *Medicinal Excommunication and Public Penance*

From what has been said, it would seem that medicinal excommunication was very closely allied to the public penitential system, and such was the case. "In the first

---

91 *Epis. 77 ad Eulalium*, MPG, 83, 1250.
92 Bingham, *loc. cit.*
93 Can. 4, Mansi, 8, 613.
94 Can. 14, Mansi, 2, 8.
95 Devoti, *Lib. IV Institutionum Canonicarum*, tom. IV, tit. XVIII, § IV.
96 *Epis.* 188, (*Canonica prima*) c. 4, MPG, 32, 674.

Christian centuries it is not always easy to distinguish between excommunication and penitential exclusion; to differentiate them satisfactorily we must await the decline of the institution of public penance and the well-defined separation between those things appertaining to the *forum internum*, or tribunal of conscience, and the *forum externum*, or public ecclesiastical tribunal."[97] Nevertheless, authors assert,[98] and it is somewhat clear from what has already been said concerning medicinal excommunication, that there was some distinction between them. Indeed, every public penance was a form of medicinal excommunication, but every medicinal excommunication was not a public penance, nor was public penance necessarily connected with the penalty of medicinal excommunication.[99]

Since the various grades of public penance were forms of medicinal excommunication, it will not be out of place to describe them briefly. It is generally agreed that there were four grades of public penitents. How early these distinctions among the penitents came into being is not certain. However, in the third and fourth centuries we commonly find them divided into four classes. The first class was comprised of the *flentes* (weeping) who, dressed in penitential garb, stationed themselves outside the church and besought the prayers of the faithful as they entered the church. The second class comprised the *audientes* (hearers). These were stationed in the narthex of the church, behind the catechumens, and were allowed to remain for the Mass of the catechumens, that is, until the end of the sermon, after which they were dismissed. In the third group were the *substrati* (prostrate), or the *genuflectentes* (kneeling), who occupied the space between the door and the ambo. After the

---

97 Boudinhon, "Excommunication," *Catholic Encyclopedia*, I, 678-679.

98 Ex. gr., Devoti, *Lib. IV Instit. Canon.* tom. II, tit. XVIII, § IV; "Magnus est etiam error illorum, qui medicinalem excommunicationem cum publica poenitentia confundunt, quasi nullum inter unam atque alteram discrimen intercedat."

99 *Ibidem.*

dismissal of the *audientes* and the catechumens, the Bishop imposed hands upon the *substrati* and together with the faithful prayed over them. Finally, there were the *consistentes* (standing) who were permitted to assist at all the divine mysteries, but could not make oblations nor receive the Holy Eucharist.

This grouping into stations originated in the East. Whether or not they ever existed in the West is doubtful. Msgr. Duchesne remarks: "The three or four stages of penitential disciple in the East were never observed in the Latin countries. We may even question, if in the East they were of universal observation. The Apostolic Constitutions and Canons do not mention them, neither does the Council of Antioch (341) nor Saint John Chrysostom. In Syria we see, both by the writings of Saint John Chrysostom and Book II of the Apostolic Constitutions, that great lenience was shown towards penitent sinners."[100]

The penitential discipline of the Church was most severe in the fourth and fifth centuries, but it was not long before it was mitigated and so modified that the four classes of penitents disappeared, and, except in extremely rare cases, public penance fell into deseutude.

It is rather difficult to ascertain unto what period the two degrees of medicinal excommunication, of which mention was above made, remained in force. However, it should seem that it was from these two grades of medicinal excommunication and the public system of penance, that there developed about the time of the Decretals the censure known as minor excommunication. Before treating of this censure, it might be well to mention here a penal measure affecting bishops (and churches) and frequently called *excommunication*, but which was rather a denial of episcopal communion.[101]

---

100 *Christian Worship: Its Origin and Evolution*, p. 436, note 1.
101 Boudinhon, "Excommunication," *Catholic Encyclopedia*, V, 679.

10. *The Denial of Episcopal Communion*

The denial of episcopal communion was the refusal "by a bishop to communicate *in sacris* with another bishop and his church, in consideration of an act deemed reprehensible and worthy of chastisement." [102]

The various churches of the Christian world were wont in two ways to show their union with the one universal Church established by Christ.[103] The first way was by exchanging letters of communion. These letters were sent by the bishops to one another, and especially to the Roman Pontiff, as a pledge of faith and unity. There seems to have been a determined formula for such letters, hence they were called *formatae.* Thus Optatus of Milevis, in order to prove that he and his church were in communion with all the Christian churches, says that he communicates with Siricius, the Bishop of Rome, "cum quo nobiscum totus orbis commercio formatarum in una communionis societate concordat." [104]

Another pledge of communion was the reception by one church of the faithful and clerics from another church. The faithful were admitted to a participation in the sacred mysteries and the clerics to the exercise of their office in other churches, if they could present letters of recommendation from their bishop.[105]

The *litterae formatae* of a bishop who was refused episcopal communion were not accepted by the bishop or bishops who had severed communion; nor did such a bishop or bishops thus communicate with him. The faithful and clerics of his church, although having commendatory letters from him, were not received into the church of the bishop or bishops who had broken off communication with him.

---

102 Boudinhon, "Excommunication," *Catholic Encyclopedia,* V. 679: cf. Hinschius, System des Katholischen Kirchenrechts, vol. 4, p. 742 ff.

103 DeSmedt, *Dissertationes Selectae in Primam Aetatem Historiae Ecclesiasticae,* diss. II, cap. III; n. 17.

104 MPL, 11, 949.

105 C. 6. 7, 8, 9, D. 71.

In the early Christian times episcopal communion was denied to bishops who were guilty of certain offences of a minor character. This penalty was very frequently employed against bishops who, without a legitimate excuse, failed to attend a provincial council.[106] Thus the fifth Council of Carthage ordered such a bishop "Ecclesiae suae communione esse contentus."[107] A council of Arles (452) decreed: "Si quis autem adesse neglexerit * * * alienatum se a fratrum communione cognoscat."[108] The Synod of Tarragona (516) deprived such a bishop of the communion of charity of the other bishops until the next council.[109]

This refusal of episcopal communion was frequently called *excommunication*, for it deprived a bishop of, or placed him outside the communion (*extra communionem*) of other bishops. Of course, it was not excommunication in the present canonical sense of the term. With regard to his church, clergy and faithful, the status of a bishop thus punished was not altered; he was merely denied the consolation of communion with his episcopal brethren;[110] he had "to be content with the communion of his own church." Moreover, this measure did not suppose in the bishop who severed communion any authority over the other. Even the faithful have at times separated themselves from the communion of their pastors, and bishops from the communion of their primates, because of a deviation in faith or discipline.[111]

11. *Minor Excommunication*

Minor excommunication may be defined as a censure which deprived one of the passive use of the sacraments, that is, of their reception. It was called minor, not because it was in itself a slight penalty; to be deprived

---

106 Boudinhon, "Excommunication," *Catholic Encyclopedia*, V. 679-680.
107 C. 10, D. 18.
108 Can. 19, Mansi, 7, 880.
109 Can. 6, Mansi, 8, 542.
110 Boudinhon, "Excommunication," *Catholic Encyclopedia*, V. 680.
111 Cf. DeSmedt, *Dissertationes Selectae in Primam Aetatem Historiae Ecclesiasticae*, diss. II, cap. III, n. 20.

of the sacraments is, indeed, a very grave punishment. It was minor, however, in comparison to major excommunication: (1) because it was incurred for offences of a less serious character, and sometimes even for venial sin; (2) because it did not exclude one from as many rights and blessings; (3) because it could be absolved from more easily.[112]

Minor excommunication had but one direct effect—the privation of the passive use of the sacraments, that is, of their reception.[113] Theologians commonly taught that one who received a sacrament while under ban of minor excommunication sinned gravely. Sacraments, however, received by such a person were no doubt valid, except perhaps the Sacrament of Penance. Even this would be valid, if no fault was committed in its reception, ex. gr., if the penitent did not know that he was excommunicated, or of the confessor through malice or ignorance did not absolve from the censure.[114]

There was a controversy whether or not one sinned by administering a sacrament while under ban of minor excommunication. The more common opinion held that such a one did not sin gravely, for Gregory IX, although he asserted that one sins by conferring the sacraments (*peccat autem conferendo*), did not say that he sins gravely (*graviter*), as he did with regard to their reception. Moreover, there was a probable opinion which held that such a one did not sin even venially. Authors who were of this opinion maintained that the words of Gregory IX (*peccat autem conferendo*) referred to cases in which one could not confer a sacrament, without receiving one himself, ex. gr., when a bishop confers Sacred Orders.[115]

Minor excommunication had another effect, which the authors called indirect, that is, the privation of election

---

112 Schmalzgrueber, pars IV, tit. XXXIX, n. 211.

113 C. 10, X, *de clerico excom.* V. 27.

114 Schmalzgrueber, pars IV, tit. XXXIX, n. 198-199; S. Alphonsus, *Theologia Moralis,* VII, n. 148; Ballerini-Palmieri, *Opus Theologicum Morale,* VII, n. 359.

115 S. Alphonsus, *Theologia Moralis,* VII, n. 149; Schmalzgrueber, pars IV, tit. XXXIX, n. 200; Suarez, *De Censuris,* disp. XXIV, s. 2, n. 12.

to a benefice.[116] One who is directly deprived of the reception of the sacraments is indirectly forbidden to receive a benefice, because the Church in conferring a benefice usually intends the *beneficiatus* to receive orders and to celebrate Mass.[117] Although the text referred only to the reception of a benefice *per electionem,* it was commonly understood to comprise also the reception of a benefice *per collationem* and *praesentationem,* because *collatio* and *praesentatio* are virtually elections, and because the same reason is present in the three cases.[118]

Minor excommunication was incurred by communicating either *in divinis* or *in humanis,* but *extra crimen criminosum,* with one under ban of major excommunication.[119] The *crimen criminosum* was the offence for which excommunication had been incurred. To contract the censure of minor excommunication, the communication, of course, had to be sinful. Hence in cases in which such communication was permissible, the censure was not incurred. However, a sin that was venial *ex levitate materiae* sufficed to bring one under ban of minor excommunication. Doubtlessly the reason for this legislation was to instill into the faithful a great dread of excommunication and to prevent them from communicating too easily with excommunicates. Minor excommunication, however, was not incurred by a sin that was venial *ex imperfecta deliberatione et advertentia,* because in such a case there was no perfectly human act, and consequently that contumacy was lacking which is necessary to contract a censure.[120]

The number of minor excommunications gradually decreased, as the number of excommunicated persons with whom it was forbidden to hold intercourse was reduced. After the Constitution "*Ad vitanda*" of Pope Martin V,

116 C. 10, X, *de clerico excomm.* V. 27.

117 Schmalzgrueber, pars IV, tit. XXXIX, n. 201; S. Alphonsus, *Theologia Moralis,* VII, n. 150.

118 Schmalzgrueber, S. Alphonsus, *loc. cit.*

119 C. 29, X, *de sententia excommunicationis,* V. 39.

120 Suarez, *De Censuris,* disp. XXIV, s. 3, n. 3; S. Alphonsus, *Theologia Moralis,* VII, n. 152; Ballerini-Palmieri, *Opus Theologicum Morale* VII, n. 362.

which left but a two-fold class of *vitandi,* it ceased to be of much importance as a disciplinary measure.[121] From that time on little attention was given to it, and it ceased to exist after the Constitution "*Apostolicae Sedis*" had been published.[122] This Constitution decreed that "ex quibuscumque censuris, sive excommunicationis, sive suspensionis, sive interdicti, quae per modum latae sententiae, ipsoque facto incurrendae hactenus impositae sunt, nonnisi illae, quas in hac ipsa Constitutione inserimus, eoque modo, quo inserimus, robur exinde habeant." As no mention was made in the Constitution of minor excommunication, which was a *latae sententiae* excommunication, canonists came to the conclusion that it was no longer in force. This conclusion was formally confirmed by the Holy Office, December 5, 1883.[123]

---

121 Boudinhon, "Excommunication," Catholic Encyclopedia, V. 680.
122 Oct. 12, 1869, (*Fontes,* n. 552).
123 *Fontes,* n. 1084.

CHAPTER III

Vitandi and Tolerati: Communication in Profane Matters

CANONS 2258 AND 2267

Canon 2258:

§ 1. Excommunicati alii sunt vitandi, alii tolerati.

§ 2. Nemo est vitandus, nisi fuerit nominatim a Sede Apostolica excommunicatus, excommunicatio fuerit publice denuntiata et in decreto vel sententia expresse dicatur ipsum vitari debere, salvo praescripto can. 2343, § 1, n.1.

Canon 2267:

Communionem in profanis cum excommunicato vitando fideles vitare debent, nisi agatur de conjuge, parentibus, liberis, famulis, subditis, et generatim nisi rationabilis causa excuset.

Excommunicati alii sunt vitandi, alii tolerati.

Canon 2258, § 1, states that some excommunicated persons are to be avoided (*vitandi*), and others are tolerated (*tolerati*).

Originally all persons under ban of major excommunication were to be shunned by the faithful not only in religious affairs, but also in the ordinary and civil affairs of daily life. The Apostles themselves taught the faithful to avoid gravely sinful brethren in all matters. Saint Paul warns the Corinthians "not so much as to eat" with a brother who is a fornicator, or covetous, or a server of idols, or a railer, or a drunkard, or an extortioner.[1] In his epistle to Titus he writes: "A man that

1 I Cor., V. 10.

is a heretic, after the first and second admonition, avoid.'"[2] Saint John, in one of his epistles, writes: "If any man come to you and bring not this doctrine, receive him not into the house, nor say to him, God speed you. For he that saith to him, God speed you, communicateth with his wicked works."[3] It would seem that in these cases the Apostles have reference to persons, who, if not formally excommunicated, were practically regarded as such. A fortiori, therefore, must the faithful have been obliged to shun the company of those whom the Apostles found necessary to separate from the communion of the faithful. This same obligation was confirmed by the Fathers,[4] and repeated by many councils.[5]

Why did the Church forbid intercourse with excommunicates even in profane matters? The following reason is given by Smith:

> The end and the aim of the Church in inflicting excommunication is to bring the refractory and obstinate offender back to repentance. Now, it is plain that nothing is a more potent incentive for the sinner to return to obedience than the fact that he is, so to say, an outlaw from society, and that he is completely isolated and cut off from all association and external intercourse with others, even in purely human affairs, namely, in the social and civil relations of every-day life. The faithful are obliged, so to say, to completely disown him and withdraw from his company, as though he were afflicted with a contagious disease, and unworthy to be in the company of his fellowmen. Moreover, the Church wishes to deter others from following the bad ex-

---

[2] Tit., III, 10.

[3] II John, I, 10; cf., Rom., XVI, 17; II Thess., III, 14.

[4] Ex. gr., Irenaeus, *Contra Haer.*, l. III, c. 3, MPG, 7, 848 ss.; Basil, *Ep. 69 ad Athanas.*, MPG, 32, 418; Leo M., *Ep. 32 ad Faustum*, MPL, 54, 795.

[5] C. of Toledo (400), can. 15, 16, 17, Mansi, 3, 1000-1001; C. of Tours (461), can. 8, Mansi, 7, 946; C. of Vannes (465), can. 3, Mansi, 7, 953; C. of Orleans (511), can. 3, Mansi, 8, 351; C. of Lerida (524), can. 4, Mansi, 8, 613.

ample of the excommunicate, by placing before their eyes the gravity of the punishment. Now, nothing could be better calculated to convince the faithful of the dread character of excommunication than the complete isolation of the excommunicate.[6]

Stringent as was this obligation of avoiding excommunicates even in profane matters, it would seem that at first it was not so rigorously enforced that excommunicates were denied the necessaries of life, or even those things which were highly useful, or that the faithful could not communicate with them in order to avoid grave danger or inconvenience. Certainly those whose duty it was to care for souls did not neglect the excommunicate: they were not unmindful of the fact that Christ ate with publicans and sinners, and joyfully did they receive back into the fold, as children lost and found, those who were sorry and brought forth fruits worthy of penance.[7] There seems to have been this distinction between those whom the faithful were obliged to avoid: those whose excommunication was public and notorious were to be shunned publicly and by all; those whose excommunication was not publicly known were to be avoided secretly and, of course, only by those who had knowledge of the censure.[8] There is a trace of this discipline in the Decretals.[9]

In the course of time the obligation of avoiding excommunicates in profane matters came to be very strictly enforced. This is especially true of the Middle Ages, as is proven from the nature and number of the matters in which the faithful were bound to shun excommunicates and also from the mitigations which the Popes found necessary to make in this matter.

---

6 *Elements of Ecclesiastical Law*, III, n. 3245.

7 Schmidt, *Thesaurus Juris Ecclesiastici, Disc. de Poenit. et Poenis*, cap. II, n. LXVII; cf. *Apostolic Constitutions*, bk. II, cap. 40.

8 Gury-Ballerini, *Compendium Theologiae Moralis*, II, n. 957.

9 C. 14, X, *de sent. exc.*, V. 39.

In what particular civil and social affairs were the faithful obliged to shun the company of the excommunicated? These affairs were summed up in the following verse:

> *Si pro delictis anathema quis efficiatur,*
> *Os, orare, vale, communio, mensa negatur.*[10]

The word *os* included all speech and conversion, whether in private or in public, whether by word of mouth, by writing, or by sign. *Orare* comprised all communication *in divinis.* By the term *vale* was understood all external marks of honor and friendship. Whether the faithful were forbidden to return a salutation was disputed among canonists. Some held that only oral salutations were prohibited and not such as were manifested by signs.[11] *Communio* referred to "every kind of daily, civil intercourse, all association in business matters, the making of contracts, the entering into partnership and the like." [12] Finally, by *mensa* was understood all constant association *per modum societatis.*

As has been said, the obligation of avoiding excommunicates even in the civil and social relations of daily life was very rigorously enforced during the Middle Ages: no exception was admitted. A wife was obliged to avoid the company of an excommunicated husband; a husband, an excommunicated wife; children had to avoid parents who were under ban of excommunication, and parents, their excommunicated children; inferiors had to discontinue all intercourse with excommunicated superiors and vice versa. Certainly it was difficult even for persons with the utmost good will to break off all intercourse in some cases.[13] It is not difficult to understand how such legislation must have been fraught with anxiety for the faithful. This was especially true when such communication became punishable by the censure of minor excommunication.

---

10 Cf. c. 17, C. XI, q. 3.
11 Cf. S. Alphonsus, *Theologia Moralis,* VII, n. 192-193.
12 Smith, *Elements of Ecclesiastical Law,* III, n. 3251.
13 Smith, *Elements of Ecclesiastical Law,* III, n. 3246.

Gregory VII was the first to mitigate the law forbidding communication with excommunicated persons. He did so in a council held at Rome in 1079. He made exception in favor of wives, children, servants and subjects of excommunicated persons. He also excused those who were ignorant either of the law forbidding such communication, or of the fact that a person with whom they held intercourse was excommunicated. He admitted necessity and even a certain utility as excusing causes.[14] These exceptions to the general rule were confirmed by Urban II in an epistle to Genebald, the Bishop of Constance, in 1089,[15] and were ratified in the decretals of Gregory IX.[16]

The causes excusing one from the obligation of avoiding excommunicates were expressed by canonists in the following verse:

> *Utile, lex, humile, res ignorata, necesse,*
> *Haec quinque solvunt anathema, ne possit obesse.*

Utile, that is, utility, either spiritual or temporal, either of the faithful or of the excommunicate. Thus, in the spiritual order, one of the faithful could help an excommunicate by giving salutary advice, by preaching in his presence, and could seek like assistance from an excommunicate if there was no one else who could give it equally well. In the temporal order, the faithful could

---

14 "Quoniam multos peccatis nostris exigentibus pro causa excommunicationis perire cotidie cernimus, partim ignorantia, partim nimia simplicitate, partim timore, partim etiam necessitate, devicti misericordia anathematis sententiam ad tempus, prout possumus, temperamus Apostolica itaque auctoritate ab anathematis vinculo hos subtrahimus, videlicet uxores, filios servos, ancillas, seu mancipia, necnon rusticos et servientes, necnon et omnes alios, qui non adeo curiales sunt, ut eorum consilio scelera perpetrentur, et eos, qui ignoranter excommunicatis communicant, sive illos, qui communicant cum illis, qui excommunicatis communicant. Quicumque autem aut orator, sive peregrinus, aut viator in terram excommunicatorum devenerit, ubi non possit emere vel non habeat unde emat, ab excommunicatis accipiendi damus licentiam. Et si quis excommunicatis non in sustentatione superbia, sed humilitatis causa dare aliquid voluerit, non prohibemus." C. 103, C. XI, q. 3.

15 C. 110, C. XI, q. 3.

16 C. 31, 43, 53, X, *de sent. exc.*, V. 39.

communicate with those under ban of excommunication for the purpose of giving or receiving alms, of paying or exacting debts.[17] *Lex,* that is, the state of marriage. Hence, a wife could continue conjugal and domestic relations with an excommunicated husband and vice versa. Could a man or woman who had knowingly married an excommunicated person benefit by this exception? The negative opinion was more commonly held, although the affirmative opinion was truly probable.[18] *Humile,* that is, subjection to and dependence upon the one under ban of excommunication. Hence, children, even though emancipated, could freely associate *in humanis* with excommunicated parents; "*pupils and wards* with their excommunicated teachers and guardians; *servants* and *employees* with their masters and employers; inferiors with their superiors; *subjects* with their sovereign or ruler."[19] What has been said concerning children, servants and subjects with regard to their excommunicated parents, masters and rulers was true also of the latter with regard to their excommunicated children, servants and subjects.[20] *Res ignorata,* that is, ignorance, either of the law forbidding intercourse with excommunicates or of the fact that the person with whom one held intercourse was excommunicated. Most likely culpable ignorance, so long as it was not affected, was an excusing cause, for Pope Gregory did not qualify the term *ignoranter.*[21]

It was by the Constitution "*Ad vitanda*" of Pope Martin V that the distinction between the *tolerati* and the *vitandi* was really introduced, although the terms *tolerati* and *vitandi* were not employed in the Constitution itself. Despite the mitigations mentioned above, the law prohibiting communication with persons under ban of excommunication was still a source of much scandal and many dangers to the faithful. The offenses

17 Schmalzgrueber, pars IV, tit. XXXIX, n. 183.
18 S. Alphonsus, *Theologia Moralis,* VII, n. 202.
19 Smith, *Elements of Ecclesiastical Law,* III, n. 3256.
20 Schmalzgrueber, pars IV, tit. XXXIX, n. 180.
21 Schmalzgrueber, pars IV, tit. XXXIX, n. 190-191.

which were punished with excommunication had in the course of time multiplied. Consequently, the number of those whom the faithful were obliged to shun even in the social and civil affairs of daily life was excessive, thus making the observance of the law difficult for the faithful in general. Hence, " to avoid scandals and numerous dangers and to relieve timorous consciences," Pope Martin V published the Constitution "*Ad vitanda*" in 1418. The Constitution read as follows:

> Ad vitanda scandala et multa pericula, subveniendumque conscientiis timoratis, omnibus Christi fidelibus tenore praesentium misericorditer indulgemus, quod nemo deinceps a communione alicujus in sacramentorum administratione, vel receptione, aut aliis quibuscumque divinis, vel extra; praetextu cujuscumque sententiae aut censurae ecclesiasticae (*aliter*: seu suspensionis aut prohibitionis) a jure vel ab homine generaliter promulgatae, teneatur abstinere, vel aliquem vitare, ac interdictum ecclesiasticum observare. Nisi sententia vel censura hujusmodi fuerit in vel contra personam, collegium, universitatem, ecclesiam, communitatem, aut locum certum, vel certa, a judice publicata vel denunciata specialiter et expresse: Constitutionibus Apostolicis et aliis in contrarium facientibus non obstantibus quibuscumque: salvo, si quem pro sacrilegio et manuum injectione in clerum, sententiam latam a canone adeo notorie constiterit incidisse, quod factum non possit aliqua tergiversationi celari, nec aliquo juris suffragio excusari. Nam a communione illius, licet denunciatus non fuerit, volumus abstineri, juxta canonicas sanctiones.[22]

---

22 *Fontes*, n. 45. "Magna controversia inde a tempore *Navarri* excitata est circa genuinum textum Const. *Ad vitanda*. Qui auctor [*Manuale*, c. 27, n. 35] diversam refert lectionem ab ea quae per S. Antoninum [*Summ. histor.*, P. III, tit. 22, c. 6, § 4; *Summ. theol.*, P. III, tit. 25, c. 2 et 3] divulgatur et Concilio Constantiensi attribuitur. Certum est agi de indulto concesso a Martino V in concordatis cum natione germanica initis; de indulto quidem perpetuo et universali ratione destinationis." Cappello, *De Censuris*, n. 142.

By virtue of this Constitution a distinction was made between excommunicated persons. The majority of them the faithful were no longer obliged to shun either *in divinis* or *in humanis*: this class became known as the *tolerati*. There remained but two classes of excommunicated persons whom the faithful were bound to avoid as formerly: these classes became known as the *vitandi*. One class comprised those who had "incurred the penalty of excommunication by reason of sacrilegious violence against a cleric, and so notoriously that the fact can in no way be dissimulated or excused."[23] The other class of *vitandi* was composed of those who had been excommunicated nominally, and whose excommunication had "been published or made known by the judge in special and express form."[24]

As regards the first class mentioned above, the *notorii percussores clerici*, according to the common opinion, notoriety of law did not suffice to constitute a person a *vitandus*.[25] Notoriety of fact was required. But did it suffice? It was probable that notoriety of law was also necessary, for it was required not only that a person strike a cleric, but also that he had incurred the censure, "ita ut factum non possit celari, nec aliquo suffragio excusari." Therefore, until the culprit had confessed or been condemned juridically, he could always be excused for some reason or other, by saying, for example, that he had acted in self-defense, that he was ignorant of the censure, etc. Hence, Saint Alphonsus came to the following conclusion; "Quare nisi saltem constet facto, quod percussor advertenter voluerit censuram incurrere, probabiliter numquam est vitandus."[26]

Two conditions were required to render other excommunicated persons *vitandi*. The first condition was that

23 Boudinhon, "Excommunication," *Catholic Encyclopedia*, V. 680.
24 *Ibidem.*
25 Cf. S. Alphonsus, *Theologia Moralis*, VII, n. 142.
26 *Theologia Moralis*, VII, n. 144; cf. Lehmkuhl, *Theologia Moralis*, 12 ed., II, n. 1128; Genicot-Salsmans, *Institutiones Theologiae Moralis*, 7 ed., II, n. 581; Aertnys, *Theologia Moralis*, 3 ed., lib. VII, tract. I, n. 48.

the person had to be excommunicated *nominally,* that is, either by name, or by so otherwise designating him that he could not be confounded with others. The second condition was that he be *publicly denounced* as excommunicated, ex. gr., in a church during Mass or a sermon, on a chart affixed to a public place, or in any other manner according to local custom.[27]

The legislation of Pope Martin V with regard to the two classes of *vitandi* remained in force until the promulgation of the Code. It is true that some authors taught that after the Constitution "*Apostolicae Sedis,*" the *notorii percussores clericorum* were no longer *vitandi.* What gave rise to such an opinion was the fact that no mention was made of such delinquents as *vitandi* in those places in the Constitution in which, according to such authors, mention of it would have been not only opportune, but even necessary (§ II, 2, 16, 17).[28] Such an opinion, however, was not sustained by the Holy See. To the question: "Suntne hodie excommunicati vitandi notorii clericorum percussores?" the Sacred Congregation of the Inquisition replied, January 9, 1884: "Affirmative * * * juxta laudatam Bullam *Ad vitanda.*"[29]

The distinction between the *tolerati* and the *vitandi* was introduced in favor of the faithful. It was not the intention of the Church to benefit those under censure. Hence, although the faithful were permitted to communicate with the *tolerati,* the latter were not allowed of their own accord to hold intercourse with the faithful. Of course, the concession granted to the faithful was indirectly extended to the *tolerati* in cases in which communication was begun by one of the faithful. Otherwise the favor given to the faithful would have been useless, since they would often have been obliged, at least *ex*

27 S. Alphonsus, *Theologia Moralis,* VII, n. 137.

28 Vecchiotti, *Institutiones Canonicae,* Vol. II, cap. IV, n. 53; Sabetti, *Compendium Theologiae Moralis,* n. 954; Konings, *Compendium Theologiae Moralis,* n. 1673.

29 *ASS,* XXXI, p. 399.

caritate, to refrain from such communication.[30] However, due to daily custom and to changes in human society, which no longer recognized the civil effects of excommunication, the *tolerati* were no longer obliged to abstain from communicating *in humanis* with the faithful. "Demum pro indole hodiernae societatis Christianae, malo fato ethnicis moribus imbutae, sapientissime S. Poenitentiaria decreto *diei 5 Julii 1867* statuit, in *humanis* juribus, nempe jure naturali et civili fundatis, *toleratos* hodie non prohiberi a communione, seu et cum ipsis et ipsis cum aliis fidelibus communicare permissum esse." [31]

With regard to communication *in humanis* with the *vitandi,* the excusing causes contained in the versicle:

Utile, lex, humile, res ignorata, necesse,
Haec quinque solvunt anathema, ne possit obesse.

were still valid. The law, however, was never any further relaxed until the promulgation of the Code. Although the censure of minor excommunication was no longer incurred by communicating unlawfully with the *vitandi,* the prohibition to abstain from communication was still in force.[32] It would seem, however, that before the publication of the Code there was a rather common opinion that the law forbidding communication in civil and profane matters with the *vitandi* had fallen into desuetude. Genicot remarks: "Rationes quas antiqui DD. afferebant ut ostenderent in pluribus casibus licere hanc communicationem civilem, hodie tam late patent ut eae vix non pro quolibet adsint. Jam vero lex quae communiter jam servari nequit, censenda est vim suam amisisse, etsi ab aliquo in particulari servari possit." [33]

The Code, however, repeats the law in Canon 2267, which states that the faithful must avoid communication

---

30 S. Alphonsus, *Theologia Moralis,* VII, n. 139.
31 Lega, *De Judiciis Ecclesiasticis,* pars. I, n. 139.
32 Cf. *S. C. S. Off.,* August 2, 1893, (*Fontes,* n. 1166).
33 *Institutiones Theologiae Moralis,* 7 ed., II, n. 585; cf. Lehmkuhl, *Theologiae Moralis,* 12 ed., II, n. 1145; Ballerini-Palmieri, *Opus Theologicum Morale,* VII, n. 411; Smith, *Elements of Ecclesiastical Law,* III, n. 3249.

in profane matters with the *vitandi,* unless there is question of husband or wife, parents, children, servants, subjects, and, in general, unless a reasonable cause excuses.

Nemo est vitandus, nisi fuerit nominatim a Sede Apostolica excommunicatus, excommunicatio fuerit publice denuntiata et in decreto vel sententia expresse dicatur ipsum vitari debere, salvo praescripto Can. 2343, § 1, n.1. (Can. 2258, § 2).

In Canon 2258, § 2, the Code lays down the conditions which are required to constitute a person a *vitandus* under the present discipline. The canon states that no one is *vitandus,* unless he has been nominally excommunicated by the Holy See, unless the excommunication has been publicly declared and unless in the decree or sentence of excommunication it is expressly stated that he must be avoided. Hence, four conditions are required to constitute a person a *vitandus.* In the first place, he must be *nominally* excommunicated, that is, he must be excommunicated by name, or, at least, in such a manner that he cannot be confounded with others. Secondly, he must be excommunicated by the Apostolic See. By the term *Apostolic See* in this canon is to be understood not only the Pope, but also the Congregations, Tribunals and Offices through which the Holy Father is wont to transact the business of the universal Church.[34] Hence, no authority inferior to the Apostolic See can render a person a *vitandus*: the Holy See alone can do so, and, it may be added, very seldom resorts to such a drastic measure.[35] Thirdly, it is required that the excommunication be *publicly declared.* This could be done by publishing it in the *Acta Apostolicae Sedis,* or by affixing notice of it in some public place, in a word, by any means, according to the circumstances of time and place, that will bring the knowledge of the fact to the faithful. Finally, it is necessary that it be expressly stated in the decree or

34 Can. 7.

35 Cappello, *De Censuris,* n. 141; Chelodi, *Jus Poenale,* n. 36.

sentence of excommunication that the excommunicated person must be avoided. All four conditions must concur in one and the same case to constitute a person a *vitandus;* if any one of them be wanting, the excommunicate is not a *vitandus.*

There is one exception to what has just been said. Canon 2258, § 2, after stating the conditions that are required to render a person a *vitandus,* adds, "salvo praescripto Can. 2343, § 1, n.1." According to this canon, one who lays violent hands upon the person of the Roman Pontiff not only contracts a *latae sententiae* excommunication, which is reserved *specialissimo modo* to the Holy See, but he also *ipso jure* becomes a *vitandus.* No declaration or sentence of any kind is required to render such a culprit a *vitandus;* he becomes such by the very commission of the crime. This is the sole case under the present discipline in which one is rendered *ipso facto* a *vitandus.*

Communication with the *Vitandi* in Profane Matters.

Communionem in profanis cum excommunicato vitando fideles vitare debent, nisi agatur de conjuge, parentibus, liberis, famulis, subditis, et generatim nisi rationabilis causa excusat. (Can. 2267.)

In Canon 2267, the Code repeats the law which forbids communication in profane matters with the *vitandi.* The faithful are obliged to avoid communication in profane matters with the *vitandi,* unless there is question of husband or wife, parents, children, servants, subjects, and, in general, unless a reasonable cause excuses. Very little comment will have to be made upon this legislation; its evolution has already been seen. The Code, while substantially in agreement with the changes made in the law by Pope Gregory VII and confirmed by subsequent Pontiffs,[36] is somewhat more lenient. Under the present discipline, any reasonable cause will permit the faithful to communicate in profane matters with the *vitandi;* a grave cause is not required.

---

36 *Supra,* p. 39.

It seems to be the common opinion that one who communicates in profane matters with a *vitandus* without a reasonable cause, and outside the cases excepted in law, does not sin gravely, unless there is danger of perversion or scandal, or unless the communication is held out of formal contempt for ecclesiastical authority.[37].

Those who give any help or favor to a *vitandus* in the delict for which he was excommunicated *ipso facto* incur an excommunication which is reserved *simpliciter* to the Holy See.[38]

---

37 Cocchi, *Commentarium,* VIII, n. 89; Cappello, *De Censuris,* n. 161; Blat, *Commentarium V. De Delictis et Poenis,* n. 94; cf. Vermeersch-Creusen, *Epitome,* III, n. 469.

38 Can. 2338, § 2.

PART II.

The Effects of Excommunication

Preliminary Remarks

Before proceeding to comment upon the effects of the censure of excommunication, it will be necessary to discuss two points that have a very practical bearing upon the effects of excommunication. The first point to be discussed will be the legislation of Canon 2232, after which an explanation will be given of the distinction between a declaratory and a condemnatory sentence.

I. The Legislation of Canon 2232

Canon 2232, § 1, states that a *latae sententiae* penalty, whether medicinal or vindictive, *ipso facto* binds the delinquent who is conscious of the delict in both forums; before a declaratory sentence, however, the delinquent is excused from observing the penalty whenever he cannot observe it without infamy, and no one can exact the observance of the penalty in the external form, unless the delict is notorious.

A *latae sententiae* penalty is one that is attached to a law or precept in such a manner that it is incurred *ipso facto* by violating the law or precept.[1] Consequently, such a penalty, whether medicinal or vindictive, *ipso facto* binds the delinquent who is conscious of the delict in both forums. Since the penalty is incurred by the very commission of the delict, *per se* it takes effect immediately; *per se* the delinquent is obliged immediately upon the commission of the delict to observe the penalty in the external as well as in the internal forum; *per se* the intervention of a superior is not required in order that the penalty have its effect. However, Canon 2232,

1 Can. 2217, § 1, n. 2.

§ 1, further states that the delinquent is excused from observing the penalty whenever he cannot observe it without loss of reputation, and no one can exact the observance of the penalty in the external forum, unless the delict is notorious. This legislation is enacted in order to safeguard the reputation of the delinquent. *Reus est in possessione.* The law would be unreasonable, if it were to demand that one betray himself and undergo infamy by observing a penalty that was incurred for an occult delict.[2] In this legislation, "we see the application of the principle that no one is to be punished unless his guilt is certain, and, in the social and public estimate, no guilt is certain unless it either has been so declared by court or is notorious."[3]

Before a declaratory sentence, no one can exact the observance of the penalty in the external forum, unless the delict is notorious. An exception is made with regard to penalties incurred for notorious delicts, because, as Sole remarks, "in notoriis nulla probatio."[4] A delict is notorious if it is publicly known, or was committed under such circumstances that it cannot be concealed by any artifice or excused by any subterfuge of law.[5] Unless the delict is notorious, not even the legitimate superior can exact the observance of the penalty in the external forum. The superior can, however, if he deems it expedient, pronounce a declaratory sentence; furthermore, he must do so, if he is legitimately requested to do so by an interested party, or if the public good demands it.[6]

The provisions of Canon 2232, § 1, must always be kept in mind when there is question of the effects of excommunication. At times explicit reference will be made to this disposition of law. However, *positis ponendis,* it applies to all the effects of excommunication. No one who has incurred a *latae sententiae* penalty is obliged to

---

2 Cappello, *De Censuris,* n. 74; Chelodi, *Jus Poenale,* n. 28.
3 Ayrinhac, *Penal Legislation,* p. 73.
4 *De Delictis et Poenis,* n. 129.
5 Can. 2197, n. 3.
6 Can. 2223, § 4.

observe it, unless at least one of the following conditions is verified: (1) unless a declaratory sentence has been issued; (2) unless the delict is notorious; (3) unless the delinquent can observe the penalty without loss of reputation.[7]

II. Declaratory and Condemnatory Sentence

Mention has been made in the preceding discussion to a declaratory sentence. Very often, too, in treating of the effects of excommunication, reference will be made to a declaratory and condemnatory sentence. Hence, it is very important to understand the distinction between them.

A declaratory sentence has place only in *latae sententiae* penalties; it is a sentence which officially proclaims that one has committed a delict and consequently has incurred the penalty attached to the commission of the delict. Since such a sentence has place only in *latae sententiae* penalties, that is, penalties which are incurred *ipso facto* by the commission of the delict, it is clear that it does not inflict or impose a penalty; it merely makes manifest the fact that a penalty has already been incurred.

A declaratory sentence is never necessary in order that a penalty be incurred, for a *latae sententiae* penalty *ipso facto* binds the delinquent who is conscious of the delict in both forums. It is necessary, however, in order that a penalty that has been incurred for a non-notorious delict have its full force. As we have seen, before a declaratory sentence, a delinquent is not bound to observe a penalty whenever he cannot do so without infamy, and no one can exact the observance of the penalty in the external forum, unless the delict is notorious.

Generally, it is left to the prudent judgment of the superior to declare that a *latae sententiae* penalty has been incurred. In two cases, however, the superior must issue such a declaration: (1) when an interested party

---

[7] Cappello, *De Censuris*, n. 74.

legitimately requests it; (2) when the common good demands it.[8] The penalty can be declared by a judicial sentence, or even extra-judicially, if it was inflicted as a particular precept.[9]

Notoriety of delict is by no means equivalent to a declaratory sentence. It is one thing not to be excused from observing a penalty and it is quite another thing to be subject to those most grave canonical effects which follow upon a declaratory sentence.[10]

From the very nature of a declaratory sentence, it follows that the penalty takes effect from the moment the delict was perpetrated.[11]

A condemnatory sentence has place only in *ferendae sententiae* penalties, that is, penalties which require the intervention of a judge or a superior in order that they be incurred.[12] A condemnatory sentence is one in which a judge, or a superior acting in the capacity of judge, imposes a *ferendae sententiae* penalty upon a delinquent for a delict that has been committed and proven.[13] A condemnatory sentence really inflicts or imposes a penalty; prior to such a sentence, the delinquent was not under the penalty; hence, the penalty takes effect only from the moment in which the sentence was pronounced. Although prior to the condemnatory sentence, the penalty may have been *a jure,* after such a sentence, it is both *a jure* and *ab homine,* but it is considered as *ab homine,* and hence, reserved.[14]

The salient points of distinction between a declaratory and a condemnatory sentence may be summed up as follows: (1) a declaratory sentence has place in *latae sententiae* penalties; a condemnatory sentence has place in *ferendae sententiae* penalties: (2) a declaratory sentence does not impose a penalty; it officially proclaims

8 Can. 2223, § 4.
9 Cappello, *De Censuris,* n. 75; Cocchi, *Commentarium,* VIII, n. 46.
10 Cappello, *De Censuris,* n. 76.
11 Can. 2232, § 2.
12 Can. 2217, § 1, n. 2.
13 Cerato, *Censurae Vigentes,* n. 8.
14 Can. 2217, § 1, n. 3.

that a penalty has already been incurred; consequently, the delinquent was under the penalty prior to the sentence: a condemnatory sentence really imposes or inflicts a penalty; prior to the sentence, the delinquent was not under the penalty: (3) from the very nature of a declaratory sentence it follows that the penalty retroacts to the moment when the delict was committed: from the very nature of a condemnatory sentence, it is clear that the penalty has its effect only from the time when the sentence was issued: (4) a declaratory sentence does not cause an *a jure* penalty to become an *ab homine* penalty; hence, the penalty which is declared does not become reserved by reason of the sentence; such a penalty, however, must be removed even in the external forum by a competent superior:[15] a condemnatory sentence causes an *a jure* penalty to be considered as an *ab homine* penalty and hence reserved by reason of the sentence.[16]

Very often in the course of the commentary upon the effects of excommunication, reference will be made to excommunicates against whom either a declaratory or condemnatory sentence has been passed as the *tolerati post sententiam.*

---

15 Cappello, *De Censuris*, n. 76.
16 Can. 2217, § 1, n. 3.

CHAPTER I.

Assistance at Divine Offices

Canon 2259.

§1. Excommunicatus quilibet caret jure assistendi divinis officiis, non tamen praedicationi verbi Dei.

§2. Si passive assistat toleratus, non est necesse ut expellatur; si vitandus, expellendus est, aut, si expelli nequeat, ab officio cessandum, dummodo id fieri possit sine gravi incommodo; ab assistentia vero activa, quae aliquam secumferat participationem in celebrandis divinis officiis, repellatur non solum vitandus, sed etiam quilibet post sententiam declaratoriam vel condemnatoriam aut alioquin notorie excommunicatus.

Canon 2259 treats of the assistance of excommunicated persons at divine offices. Assistance at divine offices may be either active or passive. It is passive when one participates merely by observing them, by following what is done. It is active when one participates in them by performing some office or duty.[1]

By the term *divine offices* are understood the functions of the power of orders which are ordained by the institution of Christ or the Church for divine worship and can be exercised only by clerics.[2] Among the divine offices may be enumerated the Holy Sacrifice of the Mass, public processions, the recitation of the canonical hours in choir, the blessing of water, ashes, palms, candles, etc., and, a fortiori, consecrations; in fine, all blessings, and

1 Cf. Cocchi, *Commentarium,* VIII, n. 87; Chelodi, *Jus Poenale,* n. 37.
2 Can. 2256, n. 1.

similar ceremonies that are ordained by the institution of Christ or His Church for divine worship and can be exercised, at least as regards licitness, only by some member of the clergy.[3] Many popular devotions, however, such as the Rosary, the Stations of the Cross, etc., even though recited under the leadership of a priest, do not constitute divine offices in the sense of our text.[4]

Under the old law, excommunicates were forbidden to assist at divine offices. The constant formula used in the *Corpus Juris Canonici* is "*excommunicatis* * * * *exclusis.*"[5] Hence, theologians taught that an excommunicated person who assisted at a notable portion of a divine office sinned gravely, unless he was excused by reason of ignorance or by the necessity of avoiding grave scandal or grave infamy. No distinction was made between the *tolerati* and the *vitandi.* The reason is obvious: until the year 1418, no such distinction existed, and when the distinction was introduced, it was done so, not to favor those under censure, but for the sake of the faithful.

At the time of the Clementine Decretals, it was necessary to expel from the celebration of Mass all excommunicates whose censure was publicly known, or else to discontinue the celebration of Mass. Pope Clement V in the Council of Vienne formulated an excommunication reserved to the Apostolic See against all who presumed to prohibit excommunicates from leaving the celebration of Mass when warned by the celebrant to do so, and also against all public excommunicates who presumed to remain for Mass when warned nominally by the celebrant to withdraw.[6]

---

3 *Suarez, De Censuris,* disp. XII, s. 1 et 2; Schmalzgrueber, pars IV, tit. XXXIX, n. 130ss.; Cappello, *De Censuris,* n. 149; Sole, *De Delictis et Poenis,* n. 202; Blat, *Commentarium,* V, *De Delictis et Poenis,* n. 81.

4 Augustine, *Commentary,* VIII, p. 177.

5 Cf. c. 57, X, *de sententia excommunicationis,* V. 39; c. 17, X, *de verborum significatione,* V. 40.

6 C. 2, *de sententia excommunicationis,* V. 10 in Clem.

In 1418, the Constitution "*Ad Vitanda*" of Pope Martin V introduced the distinction between the *tolerati* and the *vitandi*. By virtue of this Constitution, the faithful were no longer obliged to abstain from communication either *in sacris* or *in humanis* with those excommunicates who became known as *tolerati*. Since the publication of this Constitution, it has not been obligatory, at least, to avoid communicating *in sacris*, to expel any *toleratus* from divine services. Yet it is difficult to determine when the practice of expelling publicly known *tolerati* really ceased. It is certain that the prohibition for all excommunicates to remain away from divine offices was still in force and for a very long time after Pope Martin V, the violation of this prohibition, even by a *toleratus*, was regarded as a serious matter.

In the course of time, however, the force of the prohibition with regard to the *tolerati* was mitigated, not by law, it is true, but by custom. D'Annibale writes: "* * * nam tolerati (timidus dico, forte omnium primus) aut nullatenus, aut leviter peccant, si intersint divinis officiis, licet usque ad finem intersint. Etenim, cum vix reperies confessarium, qui hodie excommunicatum, his prohibeat; vel excommunicatum, qui sibi his abstinendum ducat, rigor juris hac in re obsolevisse videtur."[7] Bucceroni was of the opinion that the law did not apply in its full rigor to the *tolerati*. "Licet eadem sit lex pro vitandis et toleratis, ad hos tamen quod spectat, cum hodie vix adsit confessarius, qui excommunicatum arceat a divinis officiis, et nullus sit excommunicatus qui existimet a divinis officiis sibi esse abstinendum, rigor juris hac in re temperatus seu obsolevisse videtur."[8] Cardinal Lega wrote as follows: "Verum, ut advertit D'Annibale (I, 362, not.19) et confirmat Lehmkuhl (II, 891) hodie *toleratis* videtur permitti ut divinis intersint officiis; imo quasi hoc in votis est catholicorum, ut acatholici et mali catholici videant suis oculis sacras

7 *Summula Theologiae Moralis*, I, n. 362, not. 19.
8 *Commentarium de Censuris*, n. 99.

functiones cultus catholici et in eum, rituum sanctitate, alliciantur."[9] Lehmkuhl, in the edition of his *Theologia Moralis,* published in 1884, wrote: " * * * illa assistentia quoad divina officia pro toleratis non videtur hodie amplius vere prohibita."[10] In the latest edition of his work, published in 1914, his opinion is somewhat stricter: " * * * illa assistentia quoad divina officia pro toleratis non videtur hodie amplius tam severe prohibita."[11] Ballerini-Palmieri embraced the above-mentioned opinion of D'Annibale.[12] Genicot characterized the opinion of D'Annibale, etc., as probable, stating that "nullus episcopus increpat catholicos excommunicatos, ex. gr. Massones, qui Sacro interesse solent; immo Ecclesia heterodoxos potius allicit ad officia sua frequentanda quam eos ab iisdem removet, cum hac frequentatione crebro ad conversionem adducantur."[13] The opinion of these authors is given at length in order to show the change that was taking place in attitude toward the *tolerati.* It will serve, too, as a guide to the interpretation of the present discipline as found in the Code.

Excommunicatus quilibet caret jure assistendi divinis officiis, non tamen praedicationi verbi Dei.

Canon 2259, § 1, states that excommunicates are without the right to assist at divine offices. No distinction is made between active and passive assistance, nor between the *vitandi* and the *tolerati;* in fact, the latter distinction is excluded by the term *quilibet.* Hence, we must conclude that all excommunicates, whether *vitandi* or *tolerati* are without the right to assist either actively or passively at divine offices.

Formerly, all excommunicates were forbidden to assist at divine offices; theologians interpreted this prohibition as binding under pain of grave sin. During the last century, however, a milder view was taken by some

9 *De Judiciis Ecclesiasticis,* III, n. 139.
10 5 ed., II, n. 891.
11 12 ed., II, n. 1136.
12 *Opus Theologicum Morale,* VII, n. 397.
13 *Institutiones Theologiae Moralis,* 7 ed., n. 583.

authors with regard to passive assistance on the part of the *tolerati.* As we have seen, this more benign opinion was proposed by D'Annibale and sponsored by such authors as Bucceroni, Lega, Lehmkuhl, Ballerini-Palmieri and Genicot. This opinion, embraced as it was by such eminent canonists and moralist, has naturally led to some difficulty in interpreting the words *caret jure* of Canon 2259, § 1. Does the phrase *caret jure* mean that excommunicates are forbidden to assist at divine offices, or does it mean that they are merely deprived of the right to do so? It seems certain that the faithful have a right to assist passively at divine offices, at least in their parish churches.[14]

Chelodi,[15] Cappello,[16] Noldin-Schönegger[17] and Aertnys-Damen,[18] are of the opinion that Canon 2259, § 1, forbids excommunicates to assist at divine offices. Noldin-Schönegger and Aertnys-Damen maintain that excommunicates are forbidden *sub gravi* to assist at a notable portion of a divine office, unless they are excused by the necessity of avoiding grave scandal or other grave inconveniences.

Blat states that since no mention is made in § 1 of the prohibition which formerly existed, it seems to have been done away with (it remains, he adds, insofar as it is implied in the subsequent paragraph).[19] Vermeersch-Creusen are of the opinion that excommunicates (i. e., *tolerati*) are deprived of the right to assist at divine office, but that they are not forbidden to so do.[20] Ayrinhac writes: "He [the excommunicate] has no right to assist; it is not said that he is positively forbidden to do so. The

14 Wernz-Vidal, *Jus Canonicum,* II, n. 736; Can. 467; 1161; 1188, § 2, n. 1.

15 *Jus Poenale,* n. 37.

16 *De Censuris,* n. 149.

17 *De Censuris,* n. 39.

18 *Theologia Moralis,* 10 ed., II, n. 1002.

19 " * * * propter omissionem videretur sublata prohibitio, sed remanet ad normam juris praecedentis, quatenus implicita in § ° sequenti," *Commentarium,* V, *De Delictis et Poenis,* n. 86.

20 "Excommunicatus [toleratus] privatur *jure* assistendi divinis officiis; assistere non prohibetur * * *." *Epitome,* III, n. 461.

prohibition which used to exist is not renewed, at least not explicitly.'"[21]

Some authors have not committed themselves explicitly on this question. Sole, in interpreting § 1 of Canon 2259 does not depart from the phraseology of the Code; he employes the phrase *carere jure.*[22] In interpreting § 2 of the same canon with regard to passive assistance on the part of the *tolerati*, he explains that legislation by referring to the above-mentioned opinion of Bucceroni, D'Annibale and Cardinal Lega. He quotes these authors verbatim, and he italicizes the words of Cardinal Lega, "hodie toleratis videtur permitti ut divinis intersint officiis." He concludes his commentary on § 2 by writing: "Et ita facile intelliguntur ea quae habentur de assistentia passiva in § 2 hujus can.; quod scilicet —*si passive assistat toleratus, non est necesse ut expellatur; si vitandus, expellendus est.*" [23] Cerato does not commit himself explicitly. However, he does seem to lay special emphasis on the use of the word *jus*, which he places in italics.[24] It is rather difficult to ascertain Cocchi's view-point in this matter. After seeming to favor the prohibitory interpretation, he quotes verbatim the above-mentioned opinion of Vermeersch-Creusen. It may be added, too, that he misinterprets the words of Vermeersch-Creusen, who do not state that excommunicates (i. e., the *tolerati*) are forbidden to assist at divine offices.[25] Pruemmer is another author who lays particular stress on the use of the word *jus.* He writes: "Juxta vigentem Ecclesiae praxim excommunicati *tolerati* (omnes haeretici) carent quidem *jure* assistendi divinis officiis * * * sed jam amplius non stricte arcentur a divinis officiis liturgicis."[26]

Following the principle *odiosa restringenda* and Canon 2219, which states that in penalties the more benign in-

21 *Penal Legislation*, p. 121.
22 *De Delictis et Poenis*, n. 212.
23 *Ibidem*, n. 213.
24 *Censurae Vigentes*, n. 37.
25 *Commentarium, VIII*, n. 87.
26 *Manuale Theologiae Moralis*, III, 501.

terpretation is to be made, it would seem that § 1 of Canon 2259 merely deprives excommunicates of the right to assist at divine offices and does not forbid them to do so. The very words of the Code seem to favor this interpretation. The phrase *caret jure* does not necessarily, or even at first sight, imply a prohibition. To say that a person is without the right to place a certain act is by no means equivalent to saying that he is forbidden to place that act. A right is a "moral power, vested in a person, owing to which the holder of the power may claim something as due to him, or as already belonging to him, or demand of others that they should perform some acts or abstain from them."[27] To a right in one person there is a corresponding obligation on the part of others, at least to do nothing that will prevent the exercise of that right. A right must be carefully distinguished from mere license to perform an act.[28] Daily life furnishes many proofs of the fact that we are allowed to perform many acts for which we can claim no right in the strict sense of the term. The faithful have a *right* to assist (passively) at divine offices. The very nature of the censure of excommunication demands that persons under its ban should be deprived of this right. Canon 2259, § 1, implies that excommunicates are deprived of this right, since it says that they are without it. However, it cannot be proven solely from § 1 of Canon 2259 that they are forbidden to assist at divine offices. Just as one may place certain acts for which he can claim no right in the strict sense of the term, so one may be deprived of a right to do certain things without being forbidden to do those things.

Were it the mind of the legislator to forbid excommunicates in general to assist at divine offices, it is difficult to understand why the phrase *caret jure* should have been employed. As has been pointed out, the words do not necessarily, or even at first sight, imply a prohibi-

---

27 Holaind, *Natural Law and Legal Practice*, p. 267 (quoted in Hickey, *Summula Philosophiae Scholasticae*, III, p. 378).

28 Hickey, *op. et loc. cit.*

tion. In the very first canon treating of the effects of excommunication, no indirect, ambiguous or circumlocutory method of expressing a prohibition is to be expected. This is all the more true when it is recalled that before the promulgation of the Code there was discrepancy concerning the extent of the prohibition to assist at divine offices. Moreover, in the other canons treating of the effects of excommunication, the terms used are for the most part clear and direct, ex. gr., *nec recipere, prohibetur, non fit particeps, nequit consequi, manet privatus,* etc.: the meaning of these terms cannot be misunderstood. Certainly there must be some distinction between the phrase *caret jure* and such terms as *prohibetur, prohibetur jure.*

A comparison between the canon under consideration and Canon 2275 seems to confirm the opinion that § 1 of Canon 2259 merely deprives excommunicates of the right of assist at divine offices. Canon 2275 legislates for those under ban of personal interdict. It states that they cannot assist at divine offices (*nequeunt * * * assistere*), while Canon 2259 says that excommunicates are without the right (*caret jure*) to do so. Hence, it would seem that the former are forbidden to assist at divine offices, while the latter are only deprived of the right to do so. One might object that if persons under ban of personal interdict are forbidden to assist at divine offices, a fortiori, excommunicates should be forbidden. Such reasoning is fallacious. The direct and immediate effect of an interdict is to forbid certain sacred things mentioned in the canons.[29] On the other hand, the direct and immediate effect of excommunication is to place one outside the communion of the faithful, and hence, only consequently does it forbid sacred things.[30] Primarily, it is the right to assist at divine offices that is common to the faithful, and of this right all excommunicates are deprived.

---

29 Cf. Can. 2268.

30 Cf. Can. 2257; Cappello, *De Censuris,* n. 462; Ayrinhac, *Penal Legislation,* pp. 143-144.

Canon 2275 further states that if persons under ban of personal interdict assist passively at divine offices, it is not necessary to expel them, but that all against whom a declaratory or condemnatory sentence has been passed, or whose interdict is otherwise notorious, must be repelled from active assistance which imports any participation in the celebration of divine offices. It will be noted that this legislation is identical with that of § 2 of Canon 2259. Yet it cannot be argued from this that *caret jure* of Canon 2259 must be understood in the same sense as *nequeunt assistere* of Canon 2275. With regard to active assistance, both legislations are identical because both notoriously interdicted persons and notoriously excommunicated persons are forbidden to assist actively at divine offices. It is not necessary to expel a personally interdicted person who assists passively, because, although he is forbidden to do so, the Church for some reason or other, probably to avoid scruples and scandal, does not desire to enforce the prohibition. This need not necessarily be the reason why it is not necessary to expel a *toleratus* who assists passively; before such an assertion is made it must be proven that the *tolerati* are forbidden to assist passively at divine offices. The dispositions of law are the same, but it would seem that the reasons behind them are different.

When one considers that practically no *toleratus* thinks that he is obliged to remain away from divine offices and that no confessor or ecclesiastical superior ever enforces such an obligation, and, moreover, that the opinion which held that the *tolerati* were no longer forbidden to assist passively at divine offices was gradually gaining ground, there seems to be sufficient evidence why such a phrase as *caret jure* was employed. Any other phrase might have been construed as a prohibition affecting all excommunicates, for Canon 2259, § 1 is general; it legislates for all excommunicates without exception (*excommunicatus quilibet*). Yet, as will be seen later, the use of this phrase has not changed the law substantially with regard to the *vitandi*, who are still forbidden to assist either actively or passively at divine offices, nor with regard to active participation on the part of other excommunicates, especially such as are notoriously known to be under ban of excommunication.

The foregoing discussion has reference solely to the interpretation of § 1. It would seem that this portion of the canon merely deprives excommunicates in general of the right to assist at divine offices. If there are any prohibitions in this matter they must be deduced from the legislation contained in § 2. Before commencing to discuss the second part of the canon, however, the final clause of § 1, "non tamen praedicationi verbi Dei" must be taken into consideration.

Non tamen praedicationi verbi Dei.

Ever mindful of the command of her divine Master to preach the Gospel to every creature, the Church has always been solicitous that no one be deprived of hearing the word of God. The fourth Council of Carthage decreed that bishops were to prohibit no one, either Gentile, heretic or Jew from entering the church or from hearing the word of God.[31] When the Bishop of Ferrara asked whether it was permissible to gather together in the church once a week or once a month those under ban of excommunication or interdict in order to preach to them and to induce them to correction, he was informed that he could do so without any scruple of conscience whenever he saw it expedient, as long as no divine office was celebrated for them.[32] Another reason for the anxiety of the Church in this matter, especially with regard to persons under censure, is due to the fact that hearing the word of God is always a most useful and sometimes a necessary means to bring the delinquent to repentance.[33]

---

31 C. 67, D. 1.

32 C. 43, X, *de sent. excom.* V, 39: "* * * respondemus, quod sine scrupulo conscientiae hoc facere poteris, quum videris expedire, dummodo contra formam interdicti nullum eis divinum officium celebretur."

33 Vermeersch-Creusen, *Epitome,* III, n. 461.

ASSISTANCE AT DIVINE OFFICES

The attitude of the Church in this regard is retained in the Code, which neither deprives excommunicates of the right to attend the preaching of the word of God, nor forbids them to do so.

What is included under the term *praedicatio verbi Dei?* Under the caption in the Code, "*De divini verbi praedicatione,*" come catechetical instructions, sermons and missions.[34] In regard to the latter, it may be said that even the *vitandi* may attend them in so far as they are composed of instructions, sermons and the like.[35]

Both Cocchi[36] and Blat[37] are of the opinion that excommunicates may attend instructions, sermons, etc., even though they take place during Holy Mass. However, permission to be present at instructions, sermons and the like does not *per se* permit the *vitandi* to assist at the divine offices which precede or follow them.[38]

Si passive assistat toleratus, non est necesse ut expellatur; si vitandus, expellendus est, aut si expelli nequeat, ab officio cessandum, dummodo id fieri possit sine gravi incommodo; ab assistentia vero activa, quae aliquam secumferat participationem in celebrandis divinis officiis, repellatur non solum vitandus, sed etiam quilibet post sententiam declaratoriam vel condemnatoriam aut alioquin notorie excommunicatus.

Following the principle *odiosa restringenda* and the more benign interpretation, it would seem that § 1 of Canon 2259 must be interpreted merely as depriving excommunicates in general of the right to assist at divine offices. If there are any prohibitions in this matter, they must be deduced from the legislation found in §2. It is true that *per se* § 2 does not contain any prohibition; it

34 Lib. III, tit. XX, Can. 1327-1351.

35 Special reference is made here to the *vitandi,* because it would seem that they alone are forbidden to assist passively at divine offices. Cf. *infra,* p. 64ff.

36 *Commentarium,* VIII, n. 87.

37 *Commentarium,* V, *De Delictis et Poenis,* n. 86.

38 Augustine, *Commentary,* VIII, p. 177.

is a norm to guide others in enforcing the privation entailed in § 1. Yet from the legislation of § 2 one can easily deduce that the privation of the right to assist at divine offices extends in some cases even to a prohibition. As Blat remarks, the prohibition to assist at divine offices remains in so far as it is implicitly contained in § 2.[39] For the sake of clarity, the discussion of § 2 will be divided into three headings. In the first place, passive assistance on the part of the *tolerati* will be considered; secondly, passive assistance on the part of the *vitandi* will be discussed; finally, active participation in divine services with regard to all excommunicates will be taken into consideration.

Passive Assistance by the Tolerati

Si passive assistat toleratus, non est necesse ut expellatur.

§ 1 does not seem to forbid any excommunicate to assist at divine services. Nor can a prohibition with regard to passive assistance on the part of the *tolerati* be deduced from § 2, which simply states that if a *toleratus* assists passively, it is not necessary to expel him. The clause "non est necesse ut expellatur" indicates that *per se* a *toleratus* may be expelled. What is the reason why it is not necessary to expel a *toleratus?* Is it because the faithful have an option of associating with a *toleratus* or not, as they please? It is difficult, in fact, almost impossible, to believe that such is the reason for this disposition of law. While theoretically it may be true that the faithful may associate, or not associate, with a *toleratus,* as they see fit, yet this theory can be put into practice only in certain cases and within well defined limits. It can never be put into practice when such a course of action would cause scandal or result in an unwarranted revelation of another's delinquency. In other words, it can never be put into practice publicly with regard to occult excommunicates. Yet the legisla-

---

39 *Commentarium,* V, *De Delictis et Poenis,* n. 86.

tion under discussion makes no distinction between occult and public excommunicates; it is not necessary to expel any *toleratus*. Furthermore, the legislation has reference to divine offices, which are almost always of a public character. Moreover, since the excommunicates under discussion are tolerated by the Church, there is no reason why they should not be tolerated by the faithful in general.

It is not necessary to expel the *tolerati* who assist passively, because, although they have no *right* to assist, they do not seem to be forbidden to do so. As Vermeersch-Creusen, commenting upon § 1 of Canon 2259, remark: "Ipsis Codicis verbis solvitur disputatio olim inter auctores vigens num excommunicato tolerato divinis officiis assistere liceret."[40] The same authors, commenting on the clause, "Si passive assistat toleratus, non est necesse ut expellatur," write: "Confirmatur disciplina mitior quae jam a sat multis annis vigebat et praeclaros defensores habebat. Assistentia enim *passiva* divinis officiis, nisi in signum contemptus fiat, ad convertendos animos plurimum valet."[41] Genicot writes: "Assistentia divinis officiis *non* prohibita est excommunicatis *toleratis* * * * Immo Ecclesia heterodoxos potius allicit ad officia sua frequentanda quam eos ab iisdem removet, cum hac frequentatione crebro ad conversionem adducantur."[42]

Passive Assistance by the Vitandi

It would seem that by virtue of § 1 not even the *vitandi* are forbidden to assist at divine offices; they are merely deprived of the right to do so. There can be no doubt, however, but that they are forbidden to assist even passively at divine offices. This is evident from § 2, which states that if a *vitandus* assists passively, he must be expelled (*expellendus*), or, if he cannot be expelled, the celebration of the divine office must cease (*cessandum*), if

40 *Epitome*, III, n. 461.
41 *Ibidem*.
42 *Institutiones Theologiae Moralis*, 10 ed., II, n. 583.

this can be done without a grave inconvenience. In both cases, the Gerundive is employed—*expellendus, cessandum*—thus implying necessity or obligation. In the case of the *vitandi,* the privation of the right to assist at divine offices extends to a prohibition.

Si vitandus [passive assistat] expellendus.

The Code states the obligation of expelling a *vitandus,* but offers no special regulations as to the method of procedure. The usual course of action was to warn the excommunicate to withdraw; if he failed to comply with this warning, he was expelled by force whenever this was possible. The term *expellendus* leads one to believe that the same course of action is to be followed at the present time. The clause "dummodo id fieri possit sine gravi incommodo," which occurs later in the canon, seems to have reference to the cessation of a divine office. However, since the obligation of expelling a *vitandus* is of ecclesiastical origin, it would not bind in the face of a grave inconvenience. The necessity of applying physical force to effect the expulsion would not generally constitute a grave inconvenience, since the civil court, especially in this country, would usually uphold church authority in matters of this kind.

Si expelli nequeat [vitandus] ab officio cessandum.

If a *vitandus* cannot be expelled, the celebration of a divine office must cease, unless, of course, the rubrics demand a continuance. Thus, in the celebration of Mass if the celebrant has not begun the Canon, he must discontinue the celebration of Mass: if he has commenced the Canon, but has not yet consecrated, he may either discontinue Mass, or, after all but the server have departed, he may proceed with the Mass to the communion, finishing the remainder in the sacristy or some other becoming place: if he has already consecrated, however, he may not discontinue Mass, but after all but the server have withdrawn, he is to proceed with the Mass to the communion, finishing the remainder as stated above.[43]

Ab officio cessandum, dummodo, id fieri possit sine gravi incommodo.

If a *vitandus* cannot be expelled, the celebration of a divine office must cease, "dummodo id fieri possit sine gravi incommodo." Before the Code, Wernz wrote of the singular difficulty at the time of observing the letter of the law concerning the expulsion of a *vitandus* or the cessation of a divine office. He hinted at the necessity of a milder discipline in this matter, "ne quod in odium delinquentis est statutum, convertatur in scandalum et damnum fidelium": he added that a milder discipline seemed to have been approved by practice.[44] The Code has taken this milder practice into consideration and states that a divine office must cease, if it can be done without a grave inconvenience. "The clause '*dummodo id fieri possit sine gravi incommodo*' applies principally, perhaps exclusively, to those attending divine services. The celebrant can in practically all cases discontinue services '*sine gravi incommodo*' as far as he himself is concerned, though from a merely spiritual standpoint, there are conceivably some instances in which it would be a '*grave incommodum*' were he to deprive himself of the benefits and consolations of the sacrifice. There might be some cases, too, in which he would be obliged to continue services because of personal obligations, the nonfulfillment whereof would mean a '*grave incommodum*' to him."[45] It would seem that not unfrequently the cessation of a divine office would be connected with a grave inconvenience. This is especially true of the Sacrifice of the Mass. In this matter one must be careful "ne

---

43 Cf. Suarez, *De Censuris*, dist. XII, s. 1, n. 10; S. Alphonsus, *Theologia Moralis*, VII, n. 178; D'Annibale, *Summula Theologiae Moralis*, I, n. 360; Vermeersch-Creusen, *Epitome*, III, n. 469; Missale Romanum, *De Defectibus in Celebratione*, X, 2.

44 VI, n. 191, not. 290.

45 Motry, *Diocesan Faculties*, p. 83.

quod in odium delinquentis est statutum, convertatur in scandalum et damnum fidelium."[46]

Active Participation in Divine Offices

It has already been seen what active assistance at divine offices is. That it is to be understood in a wide sense is clear from the clause "quae aliquam secumferat participationem in celebrandis divinis officiis."[47] One may be said to participate actively not only when he performs the office of celebrant, but also when he acts as deacon, subdeacon, master of ceremonies, acolyte and likewise when he serves a low Mass.[48] Cappello considers it doubtful whether an organist may be said to participate actively in divine services.[49] Chelodi favors the negative view.[50] However, the affirmative opinion, which numbers among its defenders Noldin-Schönegger[51] and Augustine,[52] is to be preferred. Certainly an organist's part in divine offices is something more than passive. Furthermore, it is clear from the canon that active assistance is to be understood in a broad sense. Singing in the choir at divine offices comes under the heading of active participation.[53]

Not only the *vitandi*, but also all excommunicates whose censure is notorious, are to be repelled from active assistance which imports any participation in the celebration of divine offices. In order that a *toleratus* be repelled his excommunication must be notorious. Notoriety either of law or of fact suffices, for the canon speaks not only of excommunicates against whom a declaratory or condemnatory sentence has been passed (notoriety of

---

46 Wernz, VI, n. 191, not. 290; cf. Cappello, *De Censuris*, n. 159; Crnica, *Modificationes in Tractatu de Censuris*, p. 92; Pruemmer, *Manuale Juris Canonici*, Q. 571; Chelodi, *Jus Poenale*, n. 38, not. 2.

47 Sole, *De Delictis et Poenis*, n. 215.

48 Cappello, *De Censuris*, n. 149; Chelodi, *Jus Poenale*, n. 37, not. 4; Augustine, *Commentary*, VIII, p. 177.

49 *De Censuris*, n. 149.

50 *Jus Poenale*, n. 37, not. 4.

51 *De Censuris*, n. 39.

52 *Commentary*, VIII, p. 177.

53 Cf. Cappello, *De Censuris*, n. 149; Augustine, *Commentary*, VIII, p. 177; Chelodi, *Jus Poenale*, n. 37, not. 4.

law) but also of all those whose excommunication is otherwise notorious (notoriety of fact).

The question now arises whether the *tolerati* whose excommunication is not notorious are forbidden to participate actively in divine services. It is to be noted that no explicit mention is made of this question in § 2. It must be admitted that this question furnishes a reasonable objection to the interpretation given to § 1. When § 1 is understood in a prohibitory sense, the question does not arise; according to such an interpretation all excommunicates are forbidden to participate either actively or passively in divine offices. However, in view of the arguments brought forward, the interpretation given to § 1 seems justified. Moreover, it would seem that § 1 has reference principally, if not exclusively, to passive assistance. Comparatively few have a right to active participation in divine services. Those who can lay claim to such a right are sufficiently provided for in the other canons dealing with the effects of excommunication, and especially in Canon 2261.

To assert unreservedly that even the *tolerati* whose excommunication is not notorious are permitted to participate actively in divine offices would be contrary to the tenor of the censure of excommunication. Even a cursory reading of the other canons treating of the effects of excommunication indicates that no such assertion can safely be made. It seems that Canon 2259, § 2, contains an implicit prohibition in this regard. The fact that the canon speaks of repelling—*repellatur,* a rather strong term, implying, too, an obligation—notorious excommunicates seems to indicate that all excommunicates are forbidden to take an active part in divine services. The canon speaks of repelling only notorious excommunicates. It will be noted that this legislation is in strict conformity with Canon 2232. This canon states that a *latae sententiae* penalty, whether medicinal or vindictive, *ipso facto* binds the delinquent who is conscious of the delict in both forums; before a declaratory sentence, however, the delinquent is excused from observing the penalty whenever he cannot observe it without loss of good repute and in the external forum no one can exact the observance of the penalty, unless the delict is notorious. The rigid conformity between § 2 of Canon 2259 and Canon 2232 seems to imply that all excommunicates are forbidden to take an active part in divine services. However, the *tolerati* whose excommunication is not notorious are not to be repelled from participating actively. The Church, as it were, tolerates active participation on the part of such excommunicates in order to avoid scruples and the danger of scandal or imprudent defamation.[54]

Excommunicates and Obligations to Assist at Divine Offices

A very important question now arises concerning excommunicates and the obligations which may bind them to assist at divine offices. This question is of prime importance in regard to the obligation of hearing Mass on Sundays and Holy Days of Obligation. The Holy Sacrifice of the Mass is included among the divine offices at which excommunicates are either forbidden, or at least deprived of the right, to assist. Are excommunicates, therefore, bound by the obligation to hear Mass on the prescribed days?

It may be stated as a general principle that *per se* ecclesiastical punishments do not release one from obligations: no one should benefit by his malice. This is in conformity with Canon 87 which declares that by baptism one is constituted a person in the Church of Christ with all the rights and duties of Christians, unless, as far as rights are concerned, there is an obstacle impeding ecclesiastical communion, or a censure imposed by the Church. *Per accidens,* however, punishments may excuse from some obligations. This is the case when a punishment, or an effect thereof, involves a prohibition to place a certain act in which some obligation con-

---

[54] Vermeersch-Creusen, *Epitome,* III, n. 461.

sists.[55] It may be said to be the common teaching of theologians that those who are forbidden to assist at divine offices are thereby released from the obligation to attend Mass on Sundays and Holy days of Obligation.[56] It seems to be the common opinion, too, that one is not obliged to seek absolution from the censure in order to fulfill the precept of hearing Mass.[57] If, however, an excommunicate neglects to seek absolution from the censure precisely that he might be free from the obligation of hearing Mass, he would be guilty of mortal sin.[58]

Since the *vitandi* are forbidden to assist even passively at divine offices, they are not bound by the obligation to hear Mass. The question is not so easily solved with regard to the *tolerati*. One opinion holds that they are forbidden to assist even passively at divine offices. The defendants of this opinion are quite consistent in teaching that the *tolerati* are not bound by the obligation under consideration.[59] The authors who claim that the *tolerati* are not forbidden, but merely deprived of the right to assist at divine services, hold that they are not released from the obligation of hearing Mass.[60]

Which opinion is to be followed in practice? It may safely be said that both opinions are probable. Hence,

---

55 Maroto, *Institutiones Juris Canonici*, I, n. 196.

56 Schmalzgrueber, pars IV, tit. XXXIX, n. 131; S. Alphonsus, *Theologia Moralis*, VII, n. 161, n. 175; Lehmkuhl, *Theologia Moralis*, 12 ed., II, n. 1138; Cappello, *De Censuris*, n. 149; Maroto, *Institutiones Juris Canonici*, I, n. 196, not. 3; Chelodi, *Jus Poenale*, n. 37; Augustine, *Commentary*, VIII, p. 177.

57 S. Alphonsus, *Theologia Moralis*, VII, n. 161; Bucceroni, *Commentarium de Censuris*, n. 103; Ballerini-Palmieri, *Opus Theologicum Morale*, VII, n. 401; Lehmkuhl, *Theologia Moralis*, 12 ed., II, n. 1138; Cappello, *De Censuris*, n. 108.

58 S. Alphonsus, Cappello, *loc. cit.* It is to be noted that excommunicates are not excused from the precepts of annual confession and Paschal communion; they are obliged to seek absolution from the censure in order to fulfill these precepts.

59 Chelodi, *Jus Poenale*, n. 37; Cf. Cappello, *De Censuris*, n. 108, 149; Cocchi, *Commentarium*, VIII, n. 87; Cipollini, *De Censuris Latae Sententiae*, p. 58.

60 Vermeersch-Creusen, *Epitome*, III, n. 461; Ayrinhac, *Penal Legislation*, p. 121; Genicot-Salsmans, *Institutiones, Theologiae Moralis*, 10 ed., II, n. 583.

the obligation cannot be urged even against the *tolerati*. The opinion may be ventured that not only are the *tolerati* not to be forbidden to attend Mass, but they are rather to be encouraged to do so. It is by no means certain that they are forbidden to attend Mass; in fact, it seems more certain that they are not forbidden. Assistance at Mass will help to bring about more quickly the very end for which excommunication was imposed, namely, the emendation of the delinquent. Furthermore, presence at Mass may furnish the *tolerati* with the only opportunities they may have, or may take, to hear the word of God—always a most useful, and sometimes a necessary, means to bring them to a sense of duty.

Needless to say, excommunicates are not released from obligation of reciting the Divine Office. Theologians formerly taught that whenever an excommunicate recited the Office with a companion, he was obliged *sub veniali* to say "*Domine, exaudi,*" etc., in place of "*Dominus vobiscum.*" Cappello reasonably denies that excommunicates sin by not doing so. Such an obligation, especially under pain of sin, cannot be proven.[61]

No excommunicate is forbidden to enter a church or to pray there privately. Indeed, some authors teach that an excommunicate who keeps himself separated from others and prays privately in a place where divine offices are being celebrated does not offend against the censure, since in such a case there is no communication *in sacris* with others.[62]

As will be seen more fully later, excommunicates are permitted to venerate and make use of sacred images, relics, holy water, etc. Of course, they do not gain the indulgences attached to the use of such things, nor do they perceive the fruits resulting from the prayers and blessings of the Church.

---

61 *De Censuris*, n. 149.

62 Cf. Cappello, *De Censuris*, n. 149; D'Annibale, *Summula Theologiae Moralis*, I, n. 360; Ballerini-Palmieri, *Opus Theologicum Morale*, VII, 399; S. Alphonsus, *Theologia Moralis*, VII, n. 149.

At the present time, there is no penalty attached to the violation of this effect of excommunication by lay excommunicates, nor, according to the more common opinion, by those who admit lay excommunicates to divine offices.[63] Clerics, however, who knowingly and willingly communicate *in divinis* with a *vitandus* (i. e., *clericus*) *and* receive him in divine offices *ipso facto* incur an excommunication reserved *simpliciter* to the Holy See.[64] Likewise clerics who knowingly admit clerics against whom a declaratory or condemnatory sentence of excommunication has been passed to the celebration of divine offices, forbidden by the censure, *ipso facto* incur an interdict *ab ingressu Ecclesiae*, which perdures until they have given due satisfaction to him whose sentence they have contemned.[65]

---

63 Chelodi, *Jus Poenale*, n. 73; Cocchi, *Commentarium*, VIII, n. 177-178; Augustine, Commentary, VIII, p. 353ff.; cf. Vermeersch-Creusen, *Epitome*, III, n. 537.

64 Can. 2338, § 2.

65 Can. 2338, § 3.

CHAPTER II

Reception of the Sacraments and Sacramentals

Ecclesiastical Burial

CANON 2260

§ 1. Nec potest excommunicatus Sacramenta recipere; imo post sententiam declaratoriam aut condemnatoriam nec Sacramentalia.

§ 2. Quod attinet ad ecclesiasticam sepulturam, servetur praescriptum can. 1240, § 1, n. 2

I. Reception of the Sacraments

Nec potest excommunicatus Sacramenta recipere.

It may be safely asserted that if the censure of excommunication has ever meant anything, it has always meant exclusion from the reception of the sacraments. Even the censure of minor excommunication excluded those under its ban from the reception of the sacraments; in fact, this was its one direct effect. The Code is in conformity with the old law in denying the sacraments to all under ban of excommunication.[1]

The reason for this exclusion is evident. One who obstinately refuses to obey the precepts of the Church is rightly excluded from participating in her greatest privileges. Furthermore, excommunication is a medicinal remedy; its primary end is to bring the delinquent back to a sense of duty. Evidently nothing so contributes to the accomplishment of this purpose as the denial of the sacraments.[2]

1 C. 32, 59, X, *de sententia excommunicationis*, V, 39; c. 24, *de sententia excommunicationis*, V, 11 in VI°; c. 1, *de privilegiis*, V, 7 in Extrav. comm.; Conc. Trid. sess. 25, *de ref.*, c. 3; Pontificale Romanum, tit. *De Confirmandis;* Rituale Romanum, t. V. c. 1, *de Sacramento Extremae Unctionis*, n. 8.

2 Cf. Schmalzgrueber, pars IV, tit. XXXIX, n. 128; Smith, *Elements of Ecclesiastical Law*, III, n. 3195; Sole, *De Delictis et Poenis*, n. 216.

Canon 2260, § 1 states that an excommunicate cannot receive the sacraments. While the Code does not employ the term *licite,* as it does when speaking of the administration of the sacraments,[3] Canon 2260 evidently has reference to the licit reception of the sacraments. The validity of a sacrament cannot be impeded by an ecclesiastical penalty. Hence sacraments received by an excommunicate are valid, even if they are received in bad faith. An exception, of course, must be made with regard to the Sacrament of Penance which one knowingly attempts to receive before obtaining absolution from the censure of excommunication. If one knowingly seeks absolution from sin before being freed from the ban of excommunication, he lacks the dispositions necessary for the valid reception of the Sacrament of Penance; when the proper dispositions are wanting, the absolution from sins is of no value, and consequently no sacrament is received. It is clear, however, that the invalidity of the sacrament is due, not to the censure, but to the lack of proper disposition on the part of the penitent.[4]

No excommunicate can knowingly receive any sacrament licitly before obtaining absolution from the censure. One who attempts to do so sins gravely, unless he is excused by ignorance, grave fear, or by reason of avoiding grave infamy or loss in goods, and then apart from any contempt of the censure. We have said *knowingly,* because if one under ban of excommunication receives a sacrament in good faith, he receives not only validly but licitly as well. This is true also with regard to the Sacrament of Penance.[5]

The sacraments are the normal channels through which we receive divine grace. The privation of their reception constitutes one of the most severe effects of the censure of excommunication. Practically, however, an excommunicate will be deprived of the sacraments only through

3 Can. 2261, § 1.
4 Cappello, *De Censuris,* n. 147.
5 Cf. Can. 2247, § 3.

his own malice.[6] Thus in danger of death any priest, although he is not approved for confessions, licitly and validly absolves all penitents from all censures, no matter how they are reserved or how notorious they may be, even if there is present an approved priest.[7] Moreover, Canon 2254 gives confessors faculties to absolve from all censures in certain more urgent cases, namely: (1) when a *latae sententiae* censure cannot be observed in the external forum without danger of giving scandal or without danger of destroying the good repute of the censured person; (2) when it is a hardship for the penitent to remain in mortal sin during the time that is required to obtain the necessary faculty. It is to be noted that theologians teach that it may be a hardship for a penitent to remain in mortal sin even for one day. The penitent must feel the hardship subjectively, but the confessor is allowed to instill this feeling. Of course, in these more urgent cases with regard to all censures, and even in case of the danger of death with regard to censures *ab homine* and those reserved to the Holy See *specialissimo modo,* there is the question of the *recursus.* But this digression is merely to point out how anxious the Church is to have all return as soon as possible to her communion and to the benefits attached thereto. It is a striking proof, too, of the truly medicinal nature of censures in general, and of excommunication in particular.[8]

From the fact that excommunicates are forbidden to receive the sacraments, it follows as a logical and necessary consequence that priests and other ministers of the Church are obliged to refuse to administer the sacraments to them. The divine law forbids one to administer a sacrament to the unworthy. The virtue of religion demands that a sacred thing be not exposed to profanation; the virtue of charity forbids cooperation in another's sin and the giving of scandal; furthermore, fidelity in the minister forbids him to give that which is holy to dogs

6 Cf. Cerato, *Censurae Vigentes,* n. 37.
7 Can. 882.
8 Cerato, *Censurae Vigentes,* n. 37.

or to cast pearls before swine.[9] In this matter one must follow the rules given by moral theologians concerning the denial of the sacraments to unworthy persons.[10] A person whose unworthiness is publicly known is to be denied the sacraments whether he petitions them publicly or in secret: a person whose unworthiness is not publicly known is to be denied the sacraments if he petitions them in secret; if, however, he petitions them publicly, it is not permitted to refuse him. It might be added that very seldom would it be so publicly known that a person was under ban of excommunication that for this reason alone could one publicly refuse him the sacraments; usually such a one would be classed under public sinners. What has been said is true both with regard to the *tolerati* and the *vitandi.* With regard to the latter class, there is, besides the divine law, the ecclesiastical law which forbids communication *in sacris* with such persons.[11]

Both in the Decretals [12] and in the Constitution "*Apostolicae Sedis*" [13] there were penalties inflicted for the administration of the sacraments to excommunicates. The penalty under the new law is found in Canon 2364, which contains a general legislation "covering the illicit and invalid administration of the sacraments to all classes of persons disqualified by divine or ecclesiastical law from receiving them." [14] It states that a minister who dares to administer the sacraments to those who are forbidden to receive them either by divine or ecclesiastical law is to be suspended from administering the sacraments for a time to be defined by the prudent judgment of the Ordinary and he is to be punished by other penalties according to the gravity of the offence: beside, other particular penalties stated in law for delinquencies

9 Matt. VII, 6; cf. Cappello, *De Sacramentis,* I, n. 70.
10 Cf. also Can. 855, § 1, § 2.
11 Wernz, VI, n. 189, not. 271.
12 C. 8, *de priv.,* V, 7, in VI°.
13 § II, n. 17; § VI, n. 2; (*Fontes,* n. 552).
14 Murphy, *Delinquencies and Penalties in the Administration and Reception of the Sacraments,* p. 3.

of this kind retain their penal force. It is readily seen that this canon applies to the unlawful administration of the sacraments to excommunicated persons, all of whom are forbidden by ecclesiastical law to receive them.

II. Reception of the Sacramentals

Imo post sententiam declaratoriam aut condemnatoriam nec Sacramentalia.

Sacramentals are defined by the Code as follows: "res aut actiones quibus Ecclesia in aliquam sacramentorum imitationem, uti solet, ad obtinendos, ex sua impetratione, effectus praesertim spirituales." [15]

The Code divides the sacramentals into: (1) *res,* when the spiritual effect is brought about by means of blessed objects, ex. gr., holy water, blessed candles, etc.; these are sometimes designated as permanent sacramentals because of their perdurable nature; (2) *actiones,* when the effect is brought about directly as in the case of blessings; these are also known as transient sacramentals because of the transitive quality of the act of blessing.[16]

A subdivision of sacramentals which for our purpose must be taken into consideration is the two-fold division of blessings (consecrations and blessings properly so-called) into constitutive blessings and invocative blessings. Constitutive blessings are "those that permanently consecrate or dedicate the subject—person, place or thing —to God," or to divine worship. Invocative blessings are those by which God is implored to bestow some special grace or favor upon the subject.[17]

It would seem that prior to the Code there was no explicit legislation forbidding the reception of the sacramentals in general to excommunicated persons.[18] The very nature of excommunication, however, and the manner in which the effects thereof were formerly carried out leave no doubt but that all public excommunicates

15 Can. 1144.
16 Paschang, *The Sacramentals,* p. 10.
17 Paschang, *The Sacramentals,* p. 49; Cappello, *De Sacramentis,* I, n. 113.
18 Cf. Crnica, *Modificationes in Tractatu de Censuris,* p. 93.

were repelled from receiving the sacramentals. Most theologians and canonists permitted the *use* of the sacramentals to excommunicates.[19] Concerning this question, Schmalzgrueber wrote as follows:

> Permittitur excommunicato, et conveniens est usus SS. imaginum, reliquiarum, aquae bendictae, et reliquorum sacramentalium. *Neque obstat,* quod aqua benedicta, et similia habeant valorem ex orationibus Ecclesiae, quibus privatur excommunicatus; nam esto, quod iis uti non possit, ut effectus provenientes ex orationibus Ecclesiae ipsi applicentur, uti tamen illis potest in illarum venerationem, et honorem, et ut se illarum memoria, et fructus recordatione, quo per excommunicationem privatur, ad poenitentiam excitet.[20]

Canon 2260, § 1 contains what seems to be the first explicit legislation concerning excommunicates and the sacramentals in general. It states that after a declaratory or condemnatory sentence an excommunicate cannot receive the sacramentals. Hence, not only the *vitandi,* but also the *tolerati* whose excommunication is notorious by notoriety of law, i. e., after a declaratory or condemnatory sentence, are forbidden to receive the sacramentals.

It has doubtlessly been noticed that in the heading of this portion of the present chapter and in the preceding paragraph, the term *receive* has been employed in reference to the prohibition regarding the sacramentals. Some authors speak of the *use* of sacramentals as being prohibited.[21] This does not seem to be entirely correct. It seems to be their *reception* and not their *use* that is forbidden. Canon 2260, § 1 reads as follows: "Nec potest excommunicatus Sacramenta recipere; imo post

---

19 Cf. Suarez, *De Censuris,* disp. XII, s. 3; S. Alphonsus, *Theologia Moralis,* VII, n. 174; Ballerini-Palmieri, *Opus Theologicum Morale,* VII, n. 396.

20 Pars IV, tit. XXXIX, n. 133.

21 Augustine, *Commentary,* VIII, p. 180; Noldin-Schönegger, *De Censuris,* n. 40; Ayrinhac, *Penal Legislation,* p. 122.

sententiam declaratoriam aut condemnatoriam nec Secramentalia." The first part of the paragraph speaks of the *reception* (*recipere*) of the sacraments, hence the proper translation of the second part of the paragraph is: "after a declaratory or condemnatory sentence (an excommunicate cannot receive) even the sacramentals." While there is no difference between the *use* (passive) and the *reception* of the sacraments, there is, however, a distinction between the *use* and the *reception* of the sacramentals. Some sacramentals are *used,* ex. gr., holy water, blessed candles, etc.; others are *received,* ex. gr., the blessing of a woman *post partum,* etc. If it is the *use* in general of the sacramentals which is forbidden, the excommunicates mentioned in the canon may not make use of, even in private, such sacramentals as holy water, blessed candles, rosaries, etc. In this matter we are dealing with *odiosa,* therefore strict interpretation is the rule. A strict interpretation of Canon 2260 would seem to be that the only sacramentals which are forbidden excommunicated persons are those which are *received,* that is, as sacramentals, "in aliquam Sacramentorum imitationem." The prohibition seems to have reference primarily, perhaps solely, to constitutive and invocative blessings and consecrations. Such sacramentals are certainly forbidden excommunicated persons after a declaratory or condemnatory sentence. Are they forbidden under pain of nullity? Since sacramentals are controlled exclusively by ecclesiastical law, there is no doubt but that the Church could place freedom from censure as a requisite for their valid reception. In order to answer the proposed question satisfactorily, a few remarks will have to be prefaced concerning the manner in which the sacramentals produce their effects.

The majority of theologians teach that the sacramentals produce their effect not *ex opere operato,* as do the sacraments, but *ex opere operantis (Ecclesiae).* "They operate by reason of the supporting prayer of the Church. When the Church makes use of the Sacramentals she either *formaliter* or *virtualiter* asks God to grant a certain effect and it is in virtue of this prayer of the Church that the Sacramentals operate." [22]

Do the sacramentals operate infallibly? Thelogians are not at agreement concerning this question, but as Vermeersch-Creusen remark: "Magis tamen verbis quam re dissentiunt." [23] A distinction must be made between the sacramentals that consist in constitutive blessings and those that consist in invocative blessings. The former infallibly produce their effect, provided no obstacle stands in the way. They infallibly dedicate the subject—person, place or thing—to divine worship. However, "Sacramentals that consist in invocative blessings and consecrations are not absolutely infallible in their effects. The latter kind of Sacramentals, by their very nature, are destined to obtain, through the bounty of God, spiritual or temporal favors upon persons or things. Now, although it is commonly held, that the prayers of the Church, as the Spouse of Christ (by reason of which the Sacramentals operate) are never in vain and always most acceptable to Almighty God, it cannot be maintained that for this reason they will always produce the *determined* effect, that the minister or the recipient may *directly* intend. In teaching that the Sacramentals operate infallibly, authors do not restrict this infallibility as regards invocative blessings and consecrations to a *definite* or *particular* effect. For it stands to reason that God cannot grant a favor by reason of a Sacramental that would be contrary to His Wisdom and Providence, and harmful to the recipient of the Sacramental." [24] With regard to the constitutive blessings and consecrations it would seem that the Church has nowhere placed freedom from censure as a requisite for their valid reception. Hence, since sacramentals of this kind produce their effects infallibly, it must be said that they are validly, though illicitly, re-

---

22 Paschang, *The Sacramentals*, p. 32; cf. Vermeersch-Creusen, *Epitome*, II, n. 463; Pesch, *Praelectiones Dogmaticae*, VI, n. 338.

23 *Epitome*, II, n. 463; Cappello, *De Sacramentis*, I, n. 103.

24 Paschang, *The Sacramentals*, p. 35.

ceived by persons against whom a declaratory or condemnatory sentence of excommunication has been passed. With regard to the invocative blessings and consecrations, the question is not so easily solved. These sacramentals do not infallibly produce the direct effects intended. The difficulty is not so practical at any rate. Generally, the sacramental could be repeated. Moreover, in the final analysis, the effect of these sacramentals depends on the will of Almighty God. However, as far as the Church is concerned, their reception by persons against whom a declaratory or condemnatory sentence has been issued would seem to be invalid.[25] Since the effects of the sacramentals are obtained *ex impetratione Ecclesiae,* their administration seems to constitute a public prayer of the Church, in which excommunicates have no share. However, no certain conclusion can be deduced from this, for no excommunicate shares in the public prayers of the Church.[26] Concerning this question, however, Paschang writes as follows: "* * * since there is question here of an ecclesiastical penalty, canon 2260 must, according to general principles, be interpreted strictly. No mention being made by said canon as to the invalidity of such reception, the milder interpretation would pronounce the reception valid."[27]

There is an exception to the law forbidding the reception of the sacramentals to certain classes of excommunicates. Canon 1152 declares that exorcisms can be pronounced not only over the faithful and catechumens, but even over non-Catholics and excommunicates. Since the Code makes no distinction, it would seem that exorcisms can be pronounced even over the excommunicates who are forbidden to receive the other sacramentals. "Neque excipiendi videntur ipsi vitandi excommunicati, cum hic agatur de directa liberatione a daemone, cujus infestae

---

25 Vermeersch-Creusen, *Epitome,* III, n. 468; Cocchi, *Commentarium,* VIII, n. 88.

26 Can. 2262.

27 *The Sacramentals,* p. 74.

artes ipsam vim excommunicationis, poenae medicinalis, impedire possunt.''[28]

III. Ecclesiastical Burial

Quod attinet ad ecclesiasticam sepulturam, servetur praescriptum can. 1240, § 1, n. 2.

*Canon 1240, § 1, n. 2. Ecclesiastica sepultura privantur, nisi ante mortem aliqua dederint poenitentiae signa: * * * excommunicati * * * post sententiam condemnatoriam vel declaratoriam.*

Ecclesiastical burial consists in the transfer of the body to the church, the funeral services held over it in the church and the depositing of it in a place legitimately deputed for the burial of the faithful departed.[29]

All baptized persons are to be given ecclesiastical burial, unless they are expressly deprived of it by law. In this matter, catechumens who through no fault of their own die without baptism are likened to baptized persons.[30]

Since ecclesiastical burial is the last sign and pledge of communion with the Church, *per se* it is to be denied to all who have never been members of the Church, or who have publicly defected from the Church. They also are justly deprived of this supreme honor who have, as it were, deserted the Church by the commission of public and grave crimes.[31]

Under the pre-Code discipline, excommunicates were to be deprived of ecclesiastical sepulture.[32] Some authors were of the opinion that after the Constitution ''*Ad vitanda*'' the *tolerati* were not to be deprived of Christian burial, because this prohibition affected primarily the faithful and not the excommunicates, who, of course,

---

28 Vermeersch-Creusen, *Epitome,* II, n. 469.
29 Can. 1204.
30 Can. 1239, § 3, § 2.
31 Vermeersch-Creusen, *Epitome,* II, n. 546.
32 C. 37, C. XI, q. 3; c. 32, C. XXIII, q. 8; c. 1, C. XXIV, q. 2; c. 12, 14, X, *de sepulturis,* III, 28; c. 8, X, *de haereticis,* V, 7; c. 5, X, *de privilegiis,* V, 33; c. 28, X, *de sententia excommunicationis,* V, 39.

could not bury themselves.[33] This does not seem to have been true. According the most authors, not only the *vitandi*, but likewise the *tolerati* whose excommunication was notorious and public were to be denied Christian burial.[34] At any rate, the latter class would frequently have been denied it on the score of being notorious and public sinners.

The *vitandi*, even if they manifested signs of repentance before death, could not be buried in a sacred place before absolution from the censure.[35] It was not forbidden to inter in a sacred place, even before absolution from excommunication, the *tolerati* who gave signs of repentance before death. It was more becoming, of course, that they, too, should be absolved from the censure before being admitted to ecclesiastical sepulture.[36]

If a *vitandus* who died impenitent was buried in a sacred place, the place became defiled and was in need of expiation.[37] According to the opinion of many authors, however, a sacred place was not defiled by the interment therein of an impenitent toleratus.[38]

The body of an excommunicate which by accident, error or force had been interred in an ecclesiastical cemetery was to be exhumed and buried elsewhere, if it could be discerned from other bodies. If, however, the grave of the excommunicate could not be discerned from other graves, this disposition of law was not to be enforced, lest perhaps, by mistake the body of a person not excommunicated might be exhumed and buried in another place.[39]

There were penalties attached to the violation of this effect of excommunication. Those who admitted to ecclesiastical burial persons excommunicated by name *ipso*

---

33 Cf. Suarez, *De Censuris*, disp. XII, s. 4, n. 5.

34 Cf. Wernz, VI, n. 192; Crnica, *Modificationes in Tractatu de Censuris*, p. 95; Gury-Ballerini, *Theologia Moralis*, II, n. 965; Rituale Romanum, tit. 6, cap. 2, n. 2.

35 C. 28, 38, X, *de sent. excom.* V, 39.

36 Schmalzgrueber, pars IV, tit. XXXIX, n. 127; Wernz, VI, n. 192.

37 C. 7, X, *de consecratione, etc.*, III, 40; Holweck, p. 120, § 46, not. 11.

38 Cf. Suarez. *De Censuris*, disp. XII, s. 4, n. 5; Wernz, VI, n. 192.

39 C. 12, X, *de sepultur.* III, 28.

facto incurred an interdict *ab ingressu ecclesiae* and remained under it until they had given due satisfaction to the one whose sentence they had contemned.[40] Those who demanded or forced ecclesiastical burial to be given to persons excommunicated by name *ipso facto* incurred a non-reserved excommunication.[41]

Canon 2260, § 2 states that in regard to ecclesiastical burial, the prescription of Canon 1240, § 1, n. 2 is to be observed. This legislation is to the effect that excommunicates against whom a condemnatory or declaratory sentence has been issued are to be denied ecclesiastical sepulture, unless they gave some signs of repentance before death. Hence not only the vitandi but also the *tolerati post sententiam* are to be deprived of Christian burial. The *tolerati,* however, against whom no sentence has been passed are not denied ecclesiastical burial as an effect of excommunication. They may be excluded from it for some other reason, for instance, because they are notorious apostates, or notoriously ascribed to some heretical, schismatical or Masonical sect, or to other societies of the same kind, or because they are public and manifest sinners.[42]

No one, not even a *vitandus* or a *toleratus post sententiam,* who gave some signs of repentance before death, is to be refused Chrisitan burial. In cases in which public scandal has not been repaired by public penance, the scandal can be removed sufficiently by a prudent revelation of the penance done in private.[43] Signs of repentance would include, besides requesting the presence of a priest, any act of piety, such as striking the breast, kissing a crucifix, uttering an ejaculation and the like.[44]

---

40 C. 8, *de priv.* V, 7, in VI°; Constitution, "*Apostolicae Sedis,*" § VI, n. 2, (*Fontes,* n. 552).

41 Constitution, "*Apostolicae Sedis,*" § VI, n. 2, (*Fontes,* n. 552).

42 Can. 1240, § 1.

43 Vermeersch-Creusen, *Epitome,* II, n. 548.

44 *S. C. S. Off.,* 19 Sept., 1877, (*Fontes,* n. 1054); 6 Jul. 1898, (*Fontes,* n. 1200).

If any doubt arises as to whether an excommunicate is to be granted ecclesiastical burial, the Ordinary should be consulted, if time permits. If the doubt remains, the person is to be given ecclesiastical burial, in such a manner, however, that no scandal will arise therefrom.[45] Any scandal that might arise in cases of this sort could be removed by declaring why burial was granted, by divulging the fact that signs of repentance were manifested before death, or, if possible, by denying pomp and solemn exequies.[46]

One who is excluded from ecclesiastical burial is to be denied any funeral Mass, even an anniversary Mass, and also other public funeral services.[47] A funeral Mass (*Missa exsequialis*) is one that is celebrated with the body present in the church. The canon says "quaelibet Missa exsequialis," hence not even a private or low Mass is permitted. Anniversary Masses, that is to say, Masses celebrated on the anniversary of the demise, are not allowed. The term *Missa exsequialis* cannot be extended to include requiem Masses.[48] Consequently, it is not forbidden to offer Mass, even requiem Mass, for excommunicates who have been denied ecclesiastical sepulture. The application of such Masses, however, must be *privatim ac remoto scandalo* in accordance with Canon 2262, § 2, n. 2. *Other public funeral services* would include anything in the order of the exequies as described in the approved liturgical books.

Prescinding from scandal and contempt, an ecclesiastical law does not bind in the face of a grave inconvenience. Hence, when greater evils are to be feared from a denial of Christian burial, it may be conceded either wholly or partially.[49]

---

45 Can. 1240, § 2.
46 Cocchi, *Commentarium,* V, n. 71; a Coronata, *De Locis et Temporibus Sacris,* p. 268; Cf. *Fontes,* nn. 1045, 1200.
47 Can. 1241.
48 Quigley, *Condemned Societies,* p. 81.
49 Vermeersch-Creusen, *Epitome,* II, n. 550; Cocchi, *Commentarium,* V, n. 71.

Although a sacred place is violated by the burial therein of all excommunicates against whom a sentence has been passed,[50] the body of a *vitandus* only which has been buried in a sacred place contrary to the law of the canons is to be exhumed and buried in unblessed ground, if it can be done without serious inconvenience.[51] Permission to do this must be obtained from the Ordinary, who is never to grant such permission unless the body can be discerned with certainty from other bodies.[52]

Penalties for the violation of this effect of excommunication are contained in Canon 2339. Those who dare to demand or force ecclesiastical burial to be given to a *vitandus* or a *toleratus post sententiam ipso facto* incur a non-reserved excommunication. Those who of their own accord grant ecclesiastical burial to the same *ipso facto* incur an interdict *ab ingressu ecclesiae* reserved to the Ordinary.

50 Can. 1207, 1172, § 1, n. 4.
51 Can. 1242; cf. can. 1175.
52 Can. 1214.

CHAPTER III

I. The Active Use of the Sacraments and Sacramentals

CANON 2261

§ 1. Prohibetur excommunicatus licite Sacramenta et Sacramentalia conficere et ministrare, salvis exceptionibus quae sequuntur.

§ 2. Fideles, salvo praescripto § 3, possunt ex qualibet justa causa ab excommunicato Sacramenta et Sacramentalia petere, maxime si alii ministri desint, et tunc excommunicatus requisitus potest eadem ministrare neque ulla tenetur obligatione causam a requirente percontandi.

§ 3. Sed ab excommunicatis vitandis necnon ab aliis excommunicatis, postquam intercessit sententia condemnatoria aut declaratoria, fideles in solo mortis periculo possunt petere tum absolutionem sacramentalem ad normam can. 882, 2252, tum etiam, si alii desint ministri, cetera Sacramenta et Sacramentalia.

Active Use of the Sacraments and Sacramentals

According to Canon 2261, an excommunicate, whether a *vitandus* or a *toleratus,* is forbidden to celebrate the Holy Sacrifice of the Mass, to administer the sacraments and to prepare and administer the sacramentals. From the Decretals, it is clear that excommunicates were forbidden not only to celebrate Mass and administer the sacraments, but also to perform any ecclesiastical or sacred function whatever.[1]

The canon employs the term *licite.* Hence, were an excommunicate, despite the grave prohibition contained

1 C. 3, 4, 5, 6, 10, X, *de clerico excom.* V, 27.

in the canon, to celebrate Mass or to administer a sacrament, he would act validly. The reason is obvious: for the most part, the validity of a sacrament depends on the power of orders, which cannot be lost by an ecclesiastical punishment. We have said, *for the most part,* for the Sacrament of Baptism can be validly administered by anyone having the use of reason, and the contracting parties themselves are the ministers of the Sacrament of Matrimony. Besides the power of orders, there is required for the valid administration of the Sacrament of Penance, the power of jurisdiction. The *vitandi* and the *tolerati* against whom a declaratory or condemnatory sentence has been issued are not possessed of the power of jurisdiction.[2] Hence sacramental absolution imparted by such excommunicates is invalid, except when the recipient is in danger of death, or when there is question of common error. In the former case, the *vitandi* and the *tolerati* receive jurisdiction *a jure.*[3] In the latter case, the Church supplies the jurisdiction.[4]

There is no doubt but that the Church, which has full control of the sacramentals, could prohibit their preparation and administration by excommunicates under pain of nullity.[5] The Church, however, has not seen fit to do so. The preparation or administration of the sacramentals by those under ban of excommunication is illicit, but not invalid.

Like all rules, the one prohibiting the active use of the sacraments and sacramentals to excommunicates has its exceptions. It has ever been the desire of the Church that those who have been expelled from the communion of the faithful by the censure of excommunication come as soon as possible to a realization of a sense of duty, obtain absolution from the censure and once again participate in the incalculable blessings of the Christian society. This is the very aim and purpose for which the

---

2 Can. 2264.
3 Can. 882.
4 Can. 209.
5 Cappello, *De Censuris,* n. 148.

Church places one under ban of excommunication. Yet the Church has never meant by her legislation to favor those whom she found necessary to expel from the communion of the faithful. As was remarked before, the distinction between the *tolerati* and the *vitandi* was introduced in favor of the faithful and not to benefit excommunicates. In like manner, the relaxations which the Church has made in the law forbidding the active use of the sacraments and sacramentals to excommunicates were granted in favor of the faithful. The Church does not desire that the spiritual welfare of her children should suffer by the malice of those to whom she has entrusted the dispensation of her spiritual goods.

When mention is made in the following paragraphs of the licit administration of the sacraments, reference is had to the licitness of the act only by reason of the censure. It is evident that the administration of a sacrament by one in mortal sin cannot be licit. In the cases, therefore, in which an excommunicate may licitly *ratione censurae* administer a sacrament, he should strive as earnestly as possible to recover the state of sanctifying grace by an act of perfect contrition.

Under the pre-Code law,[6] the cases in which an excommunicate licitly administered the sacraments were probable ignorance on the part of the excommunicate,[7] extreme necessity on the part of the recipient, or grave inconvenience on the part of the censured minister.[8] With the exception of these cases, the administration of the sacraments was not permitted to the *vitandi,* although such administrations would be valid, except, of course, the administration of the Sacrament of Penance. Even the latter would be valid at the moment of death and in the case of common error. The *tolerati* could licitly administer the sacraments when they were asked to do so by the faithful. There were penalties attached to the

6 Cf. Suarez, *De Censuris,* disp. XI, s. 1; Wernz, VI, n. 190.
7 C. 9. X, *de clerico excom.* V, 27.
8 C. 6, C. 11, q. 32; c. 40. C. XXIX, q. 1; Conc. Trid. Sess. XIV, *de Poenit.* cap. 4, 7.

violation of this effect of excommunication. An irregularity was incurred by violating the censure,[9] and in some cases there were vindictive penalties of privation of benefice and deposition.[10] At one time the faithful who illicitly received a sacrament from one under ban of major excommunication, and after the Constitution "*Ad vitanda*" those who illicitly received a sacrament from a *vitandus* incurred minor excommunication. According to the Constitution "*Apostolicae Sedis,*" one who received an Order from a *vitandus* was *ipso facto* suspended from the exercise of that Order.[11]

The same solicitude of the Church that the spiritual welfare of the faithful be not impeded by the malice of those to whom she has committed the dispensation of her spiritual benefits is manifested in § 2 and § 3 of Canon 2261. After stating the general principle that excommunicated persons are forbidden the active use of the sacraments and sacramentals, the canon adds "salvis exceptionibus quae sequuntur."

Fideles, salvo praescripto § 3, possunt ex qualibet justa causa ab excommunicato Sacramenta et Sacramentalia petere, maxime si alii ministri desint, et tunc excommunicatus requisitus potest eadem ministrare neque ulla tenetur obligatione causam a requirente percontandi. (2261, § 2.)

Canon 2261, § 2 has reference to petitioning the sacraments and sacramentals from excommunicates who are neither *vitandi*, nor *tolerati* against whom any sentence, either declaratory or condemnatory, has been issued. They will be spoken of as the *simpliciter tolerati.* For any just reason, the faithful may request a *simpliciter toleratus* to administer the sacraments and sacramentals, especially when there are no other ministers available. When so requested, the excommunicate may administer the sacraments and sacramentals and he is not obliged

9 C. 10, X, *de clerico excom.*, V, 27.
10 C. 3, 4, 6, X, *de clerico excom.*, V, 27.
11 § V, 6, (*Fontes*, n. 552); cf. c. 2, X, *de ordinatis ab Epis.* I, 13.

to inquire why the petitioner wishes to receive them. The principle reason for which the faithful may ask the sacraments and sacramentals from a *simplicter toleratus* is the absence of other ministers. However, it is not the only reason; any just cause will suffice; a grave cause is not required. As examples of just causes which will permit the faithful to request the sacraments and sacramentals from a *simpliciter toleratus* may be mentioned, the earlier conferring of Baptism, the dispelling of a doubt concerning the gravity of a sin, the intention of approaching Holy Communion with greater purity of soul, the intention of receiving the Holy Eucharist more frequently, etc.[12] "Any reason may be called just which promotes devotion or wards off temptations or is prompted by real convenience, for instance, if one does not like to call another minister."[13]

Canon 2261, § 2 should relieve the faithful of all anxiety with regard to petitioning the *simpliciter tolerati* to administer the sacraments and sacramentals. Yet, as Vermeersch-Creusen remark, the Code, by the clause "maxime si alii ministri desint," "insinuatur obligatio caritatis qua tenemur, sine nimio incommodo, ne actione nostra alium, etiam ob ejus malam voluntatem, in periculum peccati inducamur." There is question, of course, of the sin which the excommunicate would commit by celebrating Mass or administering a sacrament, unless he had recovered the state of sanctifying grace by an act of perfect contrition.[14]

In order that a *simpliciter toleratus* may licitly celebrate Mass, administer the sacraments and prepare and administer the sacramentals, he must be requested to do so (*requisitus*). It is not necessary, however, that the request be explicit. Almost all authors teach than an implicit or reasonably presumed petition suffices.[15] Such

12 Vermeersch-Creusen, *Epitome*, III, n. 463; cf. Cocchi, *Commentarium*, VIII, n. 87.

13 Augustine, *Commentary*, VIII, p. 182.

14 *Epitome*, III, n. 463.

15 Suarez, *De Censuris*, disp. XI, s. 4; Vermeersch-Creusen, *Epitome*, III, n. 463; Cappello, *De Censuris*, n. 148; Cocchi, *Commentarium*, VIII, n. 87; Sole, *De Delictis et Poenis*, n. 220.

a petition is had whenever the good of souls demands the celebration of Mass, the administration of the sacraments, or the preparation or administration of the sacramentals and there is present no other minister besides a *simpliciter toleratus.*[16] Hence, such an excommunicate may show himself ready to hear confessions on Saturdays and vigils of feasts, to distribute Holy Communion even on week-day mornings, to celebrate Mass on Sundays and Holydays, and it would seem in these days of daily attendance at Mass, even on days throughout the week. All of this, of course, presupposes that such a course of action does not result in scandal, which, it may be added, would seldom be the case with regard to a *simpliciter toleratus.*

Sed ab excommunicatis vitandis necnon ab aliis excommunicatis, postquam intercessit sententia condemnatoria aut declaratoria, fideles in solo mortis periculo possunt petere tum absolutionem sacramentalem ad normam can. 882, 2252, tum etiam, si alii desint ministri, cetera sacramenta et sacramentalia. (2261, § 3.)

It has been seen that for any just reason the faithful may request the *simpliciter tolerati* to administer the sacraments and sacramentals. Canon 2261, § 3 states when and under what circumstances the faithful may request the administration of the sacraments and sacramentals at the hands of the *vitandi* and the *tolerati* against whom a declaratory or condemnatory sentence has been passed. It states that the faithful, only when they are constituted in danger of death, may request such excommunicates to impart sacramental absolution in accordance with Canons 882 and 2252, and also, if no other ministers are present, to administer the other sacraments and sacramentals.

There are three points to be noted in § 3 of Canon 2261. In the first place, only when they are in danger

16 Cappello, *De Censuris,* n. 148.

of death may the faithful request the *vitandi* and the *tolerati post sententiam* to administer a sacrament or sacramental. Secondly, they may petition sacramental absolution of them in accordance with Canons 882 and 2252. Finally, they may request them to administer the other sacraments (that is, besides Penance) and sacramentals only when no other ministers are present.

In solo mortis periculo.

Only when they are in danger of death, may the faithful request the *vitandi* and the *tolerati* against whom a sentence has been passed to administer a sacrament or sacramental. In the first place a distinction must be made between the *articulus mortis* and the *periculum mortis*. The former is had when death is already morally certain, or imminent and inevitable; the latter is present whenever it is prudently feared that death may ensue.[17] It would seem, however, that at the present time the terms *articulus mortis* and *periculum mortis* have the same force in law.[18]

The danger of death may arise from any cause whatsoever. It may arise from an intrinsic cause, such as disease, wound, old age, etc.; it may be brought about by an extrinsic cause, such as war, surgical operation, difficult journey, sentence of judge, etc. A norm for judging when the danger of death may be said to be present will be found in the declaration of the Sacred Penitentiary of March 18, 1912, and May 29, 1915.[19] This declaration was to the effect that soldiers mobilized for war were to be looked upon as in danger of death without further question whether they were to be sent into battle immediately.

In order to make use of a faculty granted only for danger of death, it suffices that the priest prudently judge that the person in whose favor the faculty is to be

---

17 Cappello, *De Sacramentis*, II, n. 408.

18 Cappello, *op. et loc. cit.*; Genicot-Salsmans, *Institutiones Theologiae Moralis*, II, n. 332; Kelly, *The Jurisdiction of the Simple Confessor*, p. 77.

19 *AAS*, VII, p. 282.

used is in danger of dying. When there is a positive and prudent doubt whether the person is really constituted in danger of death, the faculty can be employed validly and licitly, for in this case the Church supplies jurisdiction according to Canon 209. If the priest erroneously judges that the person is in danger of death when in reality he is not, the use of the faculty is valid by virtue of the same canon.

*Fideles in solo mortis periculo possunt petere * * * absolutionem sacramentalem ad normam can. 882, 2252.*

Only when they are in danger of death, may the faithful seek sacramental absolution from the *vitandi* and the *tolerati* against whom a sentence has been passed. Ordinarily such excommunicates are without the power of jurisdiction necessary for imparting sacramental absolution.[20] However, by virtue of Canon 882, when there is question of danger of death, all priests, even though not approved for hearing confessions, validly and licitly absolve all penitents from all sins and censures, howsoever they are reserved and notorious, even if there is present a priest approved for hearing confessions.[21] No priest is excluded from the faculty granted by Canon 882. "Anyone who has been validly ordained a priest and thereby possesses the power of orders receives the necessary power of jurisdiction for granting absolution from any sin or censure from this canon, as long as the penitent is in danger of death."[22] Hence, when a person is in danger of death, a *vitandus* or a *toleratus post sententiam* can validly and licitly impart sacramental absolution, even though there is present an approved priest.

When they are in danger of death, the faithful may petition sacramental absolution of a *vitandus* or a *tol-*

20 Can. 2264, 873, § 3.

21 Salvo praescripto can. 884: "Absolutio complicis in peccato turpi invalida est, praeterquam in mortis periculo; et etiam in periculo mortis, extra casum necessitatis, est ex parte confessarii illicita ad normam constitutionum apostolicarum et nominatim constitutionis Benedicti XIV *Sacramentum Poenitentiae,* 1 Jun. 1741.

22 Kelly, *The Jurisdiction of the Simple Confessor,* p. 78.

eratus post sententiam, even if there is present an approved priest, or one not laboring under censure. Of course, it stands to reason that a priest approved for hearing confessions, or one not laboring under censure, should always be preferred to excommunicates, especially to such excommunicates as are now in question. However, if the faithful have any reasonable cause for seeking absolution from a *vitandus* or a *toleratus post sententiam* in preference to an approved priest or one in good standing, they may do so.

Canon 2252 is to the effect that when a penitent in danger of death is absolved from a censure *ab homine,* or a censure reserved *specialissimo modo* to the Holy See, by one who ordinarily has not faculties to absolve from such censures, the penitent is obliged, after he has recovered, under penalty of reincurring the censure, to have recourse to the one who imposed the censure, if there is question of a censure *ab homine,* or in the case if a censure reserved *specialissimo modo* to the Holy See, to the Sacred Penitentiary or to one having faculties to absolve from such a censure, and the penitent after making the recourse is bound to obey the mandates of the superior.[23]

*Fideles in solo mortis periculo possunt petere * * * si alii desint ministri, cetera sacramenta et sacramentalia.*

The faithful, when they are in danger of death, may request the *vitandi* and the *tolerati post sententiam* to administer the other sacraments (that is, besides Penance) and sacramentals, only if no other ministers are present. Prior to the Code, it was disputed what sacraments the *vitandi* could administer to a dying person. It was admitted by all that [illegible] administer the Sacraments of Baptism and [illegible]ance, since these sacraments are of the greatest necessity. Many writers held that they could and should administer Holy Eucharist

[23] Cf. Pont. Comm. ad CC. auth. interpret., 12 Nov. 1922, ad VIII (*AAS,* XIV, 663).

or Extreme Unction in cases in which the dying person could not confess. The reason for this opinion is given by Schmalzgrueber: "Cum sacramentum ex attrito facere possit contritum, continget aliquando, ob receptionem Eucharistiae vel Extremae Unctionis, obtinere salutem, quae non obtineretur, praedictis sacramentis non receptis." [24]

Could the *vitandi* administer other sacraments to a dying person who had received sacramental absolution? Here again authors disagreed. Suarez,[25] however, taught that in such cases they could administer the Holy Eucharist. He argued that although in such cases the Holy Eucharist was not necessary *necessitate medii,* nevertheless it was of the greatest necessity to enable the dying person to overcome the wiles of the evil one, and it could reasonably be presumed that the Church did not wish to deprive the dying person of so great a benefit. Moreover, it might happen that for some reason or other the dying person did not recover sanctifying grace in the Sacrament of Penance, which he might recover by receiving the Holy Eucharist in good faith. It was generally held that the other sacraments could not be administered by the *vitandi,* even to a person in danger of death.[26] Some allowed the *vitandi* to assist at marriages in certain very urgent cases.[27]

The Code has put an end to all controversy in this matter. When they are in danger of death, the faithful may ask the other sacraments (that is, besides Penance) and sacramentals from the *vitandi* and the *tolerati post sententiam,* if no other ministers are present. The Code makes no exception. If no other ministers are present,

---

24 Pars IV, tit. X[illegible] Cf. Suarez, *De Censuris,* disp. XI, s. 1, n. 23.

25 *De Censuris,* disp. XI, s. 1, [illegible]8; cf. Navarrus, *De Sacramentis in genere,* cap. 22, n. 4; S. Alphonsus, *Theologia Moralis,* VI, n. 88.

26 Cf. S. Alphonsus, *Theologia Moralis,* VI, n. 88; Lehmkuhl, *Theologia Moralis,* 5 ed., II, n. 53; Genicot-Salsmans, *Institutiones Theologiae Moralis,* 7 ed., II, n. 130; Aertnys, *Theologia Moralis,* 3 ed., II, n. 27; Smith, *Elements of Ecclesiastical Law,* III, n. 3201.

27 Suarez, *De Censuris,* disp. XI, s. 1, n. 24; S. Alphonsus, *Theologia Moralis,* VI, n. 88.

the faithful may petition such excommunicates to administer any sacrament or sacramental which they are capable of receiving validly and licitly. Hence they may request Holy Viaticum and Extreme Unction, even though they have received sacramental absolution; they may petition Holy Viaticum even though they have received Holy Communion the same day; they may ask a bishop to confer upon them the Sacrament of Confirmation, etc.

The faithful when constituted in danger of death may seek sacramental absolution of the *vitandi* or the *tolerati post sententiam* even if another priest is present. However, they can petition the other sacraments and sacramentals only "si alii desint ministri." This last clause has been translated, "if no other ministers are present." A secondary meaning of the term "deesse" is "to be absent," "not to be present." "Hence by a benign though legitimate interpretation" the *vitandi* and the *tolerati post sententiam* may administer all the sacraments when there is danger of death, if no other ministers are present. "This interpretation is justified by the psychological condition of the sick person [or one otherwise in danger of death] and affords another proof of the kindness of the Church."[28]

§ 3 grants the faithful permission under certain circumstances to ask the *vitandi* and the *tolerati post sententiam* to administer the sacraments and sacramentals. In all cases in which they are legitimately requested to do so, such excommunicates administer the sacraments and sacramentals not only validly, but licitly as well (*ratione censurae*). However, it is not necessary that the petition on the part of the faithful be explicit. Thus when no other priests are present, an excommunicated priest should do all in his power to aid a dying person, even though not requested explicitly to do so.

Those who presume to receive orders from one against whom a declaratory or condemnatory sentence of excom-

---

28 Augustine, *Commentary,* VIII, p. 183.

munication has been issued *ipso facto* contract suspension *a divinis,* reserved to the Holy See. Those who are ordained in good faith by such a one are to be without the exercise of the order thus received until they are dispensed.[29]

II. The Sacrament of Matrimony

As regards the other sacraments, so, too, the reception of the Sacrament of Matrimony is forbidden to excommunicated persons. Consequently one who receives the Sacrament of Matrimony while under ban of excommunication sins gravely.

It is now theologically certain that the ministers of the Sacrament of Matrimony are the contracting parties themselves. While the contracting parties, in so far as they are the recipients of the Sacrament, are bound *sub gravi* to be in the state of grace, in so far as they are the ministers of the Sacrament, the obligation to be in the state of grace seems to bind only *sub levi.*[30]

Probably one who contracts marriage with another whom he knows to be in mortal sin does not sin by cooperation. Christian marriage follows the nature of contracts. One is permitted for any notable cause to enter into a contract with a person whom he foresees will thereby sin *e propria malitia.*[31] Nor does the prohibition of administering a sacrament to the unworthy stand in the way, even if the other party to the contract is under ban of excommunication. The position of the minister in the Sacrament of Matrimony differs very much from that of the minister in the other sacraments. In the latter, the minister acts as a public person who is obliged by his very office to attend to the merits and demerits of the recipients, lest he become an unfaithful dispenser; in the Sacrament of Matrimony, on the con-

29 Can. 2372; cf. *supra,* p. 73; *infra,* pp. 165-166.

30 Genicot-Salsmans, *Institutiones Theologiae Moralis,* 10 ed., II, n. 115; Cappello, *De Sacramentis,* III, n. 37; Wernz-Vidal, *Jus Canonicum,* V, n. 202.

31 Genicot-Salsmans, II, n. 464; I, n. 233.

trary, the minister is a private person entering into a contract and hence he attends only to his own utility.[82] Genicot-Salsmans remark, however, that it seems to be a grave sin to contract marriage with a *vitandus*.[83]

1. *Assistance at Marriage*

Assistance at marriage entails neither the administration of a sacrament, nor an exercise of the power of jurisdiction. It is very closely allied, however, to the latter, because the right to assist at marriage is acquired by virtue of an office and because the right can be delegated.[84] Since, however, assistance at marriage is likewise very closely connected with the administration of the sacraments, it was thought more advisable to treat of the few points which bear upon the subject of this dissertation in connection with the administration of the sacraments than with the exercise of the power of jurisdiction. Two points will be discussed. The first will concern assistance at the marriage of notoriously excommunicated persons. The second will treat of assistance at marriage on the part of excommunicated priests.

(A) *Assistance at the Marriage of Notorious Excommunicates*

CANON 1066.

Si publicus peccator aut censura notorie innodatus prius ad sacramentalem confessionem accedere aut cum Ecclesia reconciliari recusaverit, parochus ejus matrimonio ne assistat, nisi gravis urgeat causa, de qua, si fieri possit, consulat Ordinarium.

Canon 1066 states that if a public sinner, or one notoriously under ban of censure, refuses first to approach sacramental confession or to be reconciled with the Church, the pastor is not to assist at his marriage, unless a grave cause urges, concerning which, if possible,

82 Genicot-Salsmans, II, n. 464.

83 *Ibidem*, not. 1.

84 Cappello, *De Sacramentis*, III, n. 649.

he is to consult the Ordinary. Our commentary on this canon will be confined to assistance at the marriages of persons who are notoriously under ban of excommunication.

Persons who are notorious excommunicates are enumerated among the *indigni*. In the first place, it is to be noted that the legislation takes cognizance only of notorious excommunicates. If the fact that a person is under ban of excommunication is known only through the confessional, it cannot be taken into consideration in the external forum. If although known outside the confessional, a person's excommunication remains occult, the pastor is obliged to warn such a one privately of the obligation of becoming reconciled with the Church, unless, of course, the pastor prudently judges that it is more expedient to abstain from admonition.[85] However, the pastor can and must assist at the marriage of such a person.[86]

The censure of excommunication may be notorious by notoriety either of law or of fact. It is notorious by notoriety of law after a declaratory or condemnatory sentence. It is notorious by notoriety of fact when a delict, which is publicly known to be punished by excommunication, is committed under such circumstances that it cannot be concealed by any artifice or excused by any subterfuge of law.[87] Notoriety either of law or of fact suffices to bring an excommunicate under the legislation of Canon 1066.[88]

Before being admitted to contract marriage, a notorious excommunicate must first be reconciled with the Church, that is, he must obtain absolution from the censure. A censure is a vinculum of the external forum. Hence *per se* it must be removed in that forum. Absolution granted in the external forum affects both forums.

85 Wernz-Vidal, *Jus Canonicum*, V, n. 202; Ayrinhac, *Marriage Legislation in the New Code*, p. 132.

86 Wernz-Vidal, *loc. cit.;* Cappello, *De Sacramentis*, III, n. 332; DeSmet, *De Sponsalibus et Matrimonio*, n. 194.

87 Can. 2197.

88 DeSmet, *De Sponsalibus et Matrimonio*, n. 195, not. 5.

However, when absolution has been obtained in the internal forum, one may, if scandal is removed, conduct himself as absolved even in the external forum, but unless the absolution is proved or at least legitimately presumed in the external forum, the censure can be enforced by the superior having jurisdiction in the external forum, and the censured one is obliged to obey.[39] However, in cases in which absolution in the internal forum can be legitimately presumed, the superior of the external forum can accept such an absolution for the external forum also.[40]

Wernz-Vidal are of the opinion that notorious excommunicates are to be dealt with in the same manner as public sinners, that is, they must approach sacramental confession, "dum non constat per absolutionem a censura fuisse cum Ecclesia reconciliatum."[41] To preclude the danger of scandal, it is always required that the fact of reconciliation be established by an act publicly posited, or by the divulgation of such an act.[42]

If a notorious excommunicate refuses to be reconciled with the Church, the pastor is not to assist at his marriage, unless a grave cause urges, concerning which, if it is possible, he is to consult the Ordinary. Assistance at the marriage of such a person is not intrinsically evil; hence it can be permitted for proportionately grave causes. Among grave causes which would permit assistance at such marriages may be mentioned the following: if the parties have already contracted marriage civilly, or there is danger that they might do so; if it is very difficult for the innocent party to relinquish the marriage; or generally, if all things considered, greater evils would follow upon a refusal to assist at such a marriage.[43] Practically all authors demand a much graver

39 Can. 2251.

40 Cocchi, *Commentarium*, VIII, n. 76; Cappello, *De Censuris*, n. 98; Sole, *De Delictis et Poenis*, n. 185.

41 *Jus Canonicum*, V, n. 202.

42 *Ibidem.*

43 Cf. Wernz-Vidal, Cappello, DeSmet, *loc. cit.*

cause to permit assistance at the marriage of an excommunicate who is a *vitandus* or a *toleratus* against whom a declaratory or condemnatory sentence has been issued.[44] Gasparri, Chelodi and Cappello require a *causa gravissima* to permit assistance at the marriage of a *vitandus.*[45]

(B) *Assistance at Marriage by Excommunicated Priests*

CANON 1095.

§ 1. Parochus et loci Ordinarius valide matrimonio assistunt:

*1.° * * * nisi per sententiam fuerint excommunicati * * * aut tales declarati.*

§ 2. Parochus et loci Ordinarius qui matrimonio possunt valide assistere, possunt quoque alii sacerdoti licentiam dare ut intra fines sui territorii matrimonio valide assistat.

It has been pointed out that the right to assist at marriages is very similar to the exercise of the power of jurisdiction; it is obtained by virtue of an office and it can be delegated to others. It has another likeness to the power of jurisdiction. In ordinary circumstances, acts of jurisdiction cannot validly be placed by persons against whom a declaratory or condemnatory sentence of excommunication has been issued.[46] In like manner, a pastor and local Ordinary cannot validly assist at marriage after a declaratory or condemnatory sentence of excommunication ("per sententiam fuerint excommunicati * * * aut tales declarati.")[47] It is to be noted that if a pastor or local Ordinary should unfortunately become a *vitandus,* he would *ipso facto* be deprived of his

---

44 Gasparri, *De Matrimonio,* n. 536; Chelodi, *Jus Matrimoniale,* n. 67; Cappello, *De Sacramentis,* III, n. 332; Wernz-Vidal, *Jus Canonicum,* V, n. 202; Farrugia, *De Matrimonio et Causis Matrimonialibus,* n. 142.

45 *Loc. cit.*

46 Can. 2264.

47 Can. 1095, § 1, n. 1.

office as pastor or Ordinary and consequently could not validly assist at marriages.[48]

An excommunicated pastor or local Ordinary, against whom no sentence has been issued, can assist validly at marriages, provided, of course, that all the other requisites mentioned in Canon 1095, § 1, nn. 1, 2, 3, are verified. Can such a one do so licitly? It would seem that he cannot. Assistance at marriage, it is true, does not constitute an administration of a sacrament, still it does entail active use of the sacramentals, which is forbidden to all excommunicates by virtue of Canon 2261. In this, as in all similar cases, however, the provisions of Canon 2232 must be borne in mind: before a declaratory sentence, one is not obliged to observe a *latae sententiae* penalty, whenever he cannot do so without loss of good repute.

The pastor and local Ordinary who can validly assist at marriage can likewise give permission to another priest to assist validly at marriage within their territory.[49] It is to be noted that Canon 1095, § 2 states explicitly that permission can be given by the pastor and local Ordinary "qui matrimonio possunt valide assistere." Since the pastor and local Ordinary against whom a declaratory or condemnatory sentence has been passed cannot validly assist at marriage, they cannot validly grant permission to another priest to do so. This is evidently the meaning of Canon 1095, § 2, and is the opinion commonly accepted by canonists.[50] This view-point is in accordance with the principle: *Nemo potest plus juris transferre in alium quam sibi competere dignoscatur.*[51]

Can a pastor or local Ordinary give permission to assist at marriage to a priest against whom a declaratory or condemnatory sentence of excommunication has been

---

48 Can. 2266.

49 Can 1095, § 2.

50 Wernz-Vidal, *Jus Canonicum,* V, n. 538; Cappello, *De Sacramentis,* III, n. 673; Chelodi, *Jus Matrimoniale,* n. 133; Vlaming, *Praelectiones Juris Matrimonii,* n. 572; Linneborn, *Grundriss des Eherechts nach dem C. J. C.,* p. 321; Petrovits, *The New Church Law on Matrimony,* n. 468.

51 Reg. 79, *Regulae Juris* in VI°.

passed? In the first place, no pastor or local Ordinary can do so *licitly*, for no excommunicate can licitly assist at marriage, since it entails active use of the sacramentals.[52] It would seem that a pastor or local Ordinary cannot do so even *validly*.[53] It is the common teaching of canonists that the delegated priest, similar to the pastor and local Ordinary, must not be forced to assist by grave violence or fear and that he must ask and receive the consent of the contracting parties; furthermore, a delegated priest cannot validly assist at marriage outside the territory of the pastor or Ordinary who delegates him.[54] *A pari*, therefore, it would seem that a delegated priest who is a *post sententiam* excommunicate cannot validly assist at marriage. Moreover, under the *Ne Temere* legislation, the delegated priest, in order to assist validly and licitly, was obliged to observe the limits of his mandate and the rules laid down for valid and licit assistance on the part of the pastor and Ordinary.[55] Hence, a delegated priest who had been nominally excommunicated in a public decree could not validly assist at marriage. It would seem that under the discipline of the Code, the rules laid down for valid assistance on the part of the pastor and Ordinary must be observed by a delegated priest, although the Code does not expressly say so.[56]

Vlaming, however, maintains that immunity from censure according to Canon 1095, § 1, n. 2 is not required in the delegated priest. He writes: "Immunitas a censura, ad normam can. 1095, § 1, 2° requiritur quidem in delegante, ceu teste qualificato *ordinario*, sed nullibi in delegato, qui est testis qualificatus *extra-ordinarius*, ideoque paritate cum illo carens."[57] Petrovits embraced this

---

52 Can. 2261.

53 DeSmet, *De Sponsalibus et Matrimonio*, n. 122; Vermeersch-Creusen, *Epitome*, II, n. 396; Linneborn, *Grundriss des Eherechts nach dem C. J. C.*, p. 321.

54 Cf. Can. 1095, § 1, n. 2, 3.

55 Decretum *Ne Temere*, IV, V, VI.

56 DeSmet, *De Sponsalibus et Matrimonio*, n. 122.

57 *Praelectiones Juris Matrimonii*, n. 573, not. 2.

opinion in the first edition of his work.[58] He rejects it, however, in his second edition. Without making any reference to validity or invalidity, he states that such a priest *may* not be delegated "nor may he presume to perform such an act except for one who is in danger of death *et alii desint ministri.*"[59]

Concerning this question there would seem to be a doubt of law (*dubium juris*).

2. *Matrimonial Dispensations*

It will be necessary to touch upon a few points relative to matrimonial dispensations. The granting of a dispensation is an exercise of the power of jurisdiction. Hence, ordinarily, the granting of matrimonial dispensations should be considered under Canon 2264. However, to maintain unity of subject, it was deemed more advisable to discuss the granting of matrimonial dispensations by excommunicates in this place. Two points will be discussed. The first will concern the *vitandi* and the *tolerati post sententiam* as the confessor of Canon 1044. The second point will bear upon the same classes of excommunicates as the priest who assists at marriage in virtue of Canon 1098, n. 2.

(A) *The Vitandi and the Tolerati post sententiam as the Confessor of Canon 1044*

Since even the *vitandi* and the *tolerati post sententiam* may hear the confession of any person who is in danger of death, so, too, when necessary, they may make use of the faculty of dispensing granted by Canon 1044.[60] In order better to understand the faculty granted by Canon 1044, it will be necessary to quote Canon 1043, of which Canon 1044 is but an extention. Canon 1043 states that in (urgent) danger of death, in order to soothe conscience, and, if the case warrants it, to legitimatize the

---

58 *The New Church Law on Matrimony,* (1921), n. 474.

59 *The New Church Law on Matrimony,* (1926), n. 474.

60 Cf. Cappello, *De Sacramentis,* III, n. 238; Kelly, *The Jurisdiction of the Simple Confessor,* p. 84.

offspring, local Ordinaries can dispense from the form prescribed for the celebration of marriage and likewise from all impediments of ecclesiastical law, whether they are public or occult, even if they are multiple, with the exceptions of the impediment arising from Sacred Priesthood and the impediment arising from affinity in the direct line, when the marriage has been consummated; local Ordinaries can use this faculty in favor of their own subjects wherever the subjects may be, and also in favor of all who are actually within their territory; scandal must be avoided; and if a dispensation is granted from the impediment of disparity of cult or of mixed religion, the customary promises are to be given. Under the same circumstances, and for cases in which the local Ordinary cannot be approached, Canon 1044 extends the same faculty of dispensing to the pastor, the priest who assists at the marriage in virtue of Canon 1098, n. 2, and the *confessor;* the confessor, however, can exercise this power of dispensing for the internal forum and in the act of sacramental confession only. Since Canon 1044 has no direct bearing upon the subject-matter of this dissertation, no attempt will be made to enter into an explanation of the many debatable questions that arise in connection with it. For such, the reader is referred to authors who treat specifically of the matrimonial legislation.

(B) *The Vitandi and the Tolerati post sententiam as the Priest who Assists at Marriage in Virtue of Canon 1098, n. 2*

If the pastor, or the Ordinary, or a priest delegated by either, cannot be had or approached without grave inconvenience, marriage may be contracted both validly and licitly in the presence of witnesses only: (1) when at least one of the parties is in danger of death; (2) when it is prudently foreseen that the same state of affairs (absence of competent priest) will last for a month. In either case, if another priest is at hand who is able to be present, he ought (*debet*) to be called and assist at the marriage together with the witnesses; under the circumstances, however, the presence of the witnesses only is required for the validity of the marriage.[61]

Is there any *obligation* to call an excommunicated priest to assist at the marriage, if such a one is the only priest at hand? There is some division among canonists on this point. Vlaming,[62] DeSmet,[63] Vermeersch-Creusen [64] and Cappello [65] are of the opinion that the obligation does not hold, if the only priest at hand is a *vitandus*. DeSmet and Cappello favor the same viewpoint with regard to the *tolerati post sententiam*. Leitner claims that there is no obligation to call in any censured priest.[66] Cerato, however, holds that the priest is to be called, even though he is excommunicated *per sententiam*.[67] Petrovits writes: "The words *alius sacerdos* permit the inference that the obligation to request the presence of a priest would not be removed even if the parties were constrained to use the services of one who is excommunicated * * *.[68] Augustine says that the priest spoken of in Canon 1098, n. 2, "may be any priest, even one under censure." [69]

Certainly the opinion of such canonists as Vlaming, DeSmet, Cappello, Vermeersch-Creusen and Leitner constitutes sufficient authority to free the parties from the obligation, light as it is, imposed by Canon 1098, n. 2, of calling in a *vitandus*. Hence, when the only priest

---

61 Canon 1098, nn. 1, 2. This canon is to be understood as referring only to the physical absence of the pastor or local Ordinary. Pont. Comm., March 10, 1928, (*AAS*, XX, p. 120).

62 "Conditio non videtur urgere * * * probabilius si, qui praesto habetur sacerdos, sit excommunicatus vitandus." *Praelectiones Juris Matrimonii*, n. 586.

63 "Dicitur: alius sacerdos, sine ulla restrictione; merito tamen dices quod, si nupturientes, attento can. 2261, § 3, possent, non tamen deberent recurrere ad sacerdotem qui, per sententiam sit excommunicatus." *De Sponsalibus et Matrimonio*, n. 134, not. 1.

64 *Epitome*, II, n. 406.

65 *De Sacramentis*, III, n. 696.

66 *Lehrbuch des katholischen Eherechts*, p. 207.

67 *Matrimonium a Codice Juris Canonici integre Desumptum*, n. 95.

68 *The New Church Law on Matrimony*, n. 501.

69 *Commentary*, V, p. 925.

available is a *vitandus, per se* the parties are not obliged to call upon him to assist at the marriage. Most likely the same should be held with Cappello and DeSmet with regard to the *tolerati post sententiam.* After all, the Code, in the canons treating of the effects of excommunication, points out rather clearly that the proper distinction to make in these matters is not between the *tolerati* and the *vitandi,* but rather between the *simpliciter tolerati* on the one hand and the *vitandi* and the *tolerati post sententiam* on the other.

Thus far, the discussion has been whether a *vitandus* or a *toleratus* against whom a declaratory or condemnatory sentence has been passed *must* be called upon to assist at a marriage in conformity with Canon 1098, n. 2. The question now arises whether such a priest *may* be called upon to do so, when no other priests are available. It is certain that when one of the parties is in danger of death, such a priest may be called upon to assist at a marriage in order to bless it and to administer the other sacramentals that have place in the Catholic celebration of marriage.[70]

May such excommunicates be called upon to assist at a marriage in the other case that comes under Canon 1098, that is, when it is prudently foreseen that a competent priest will not be had for a month? It would seem that they may not. Canon 2261, § 3 states explicitly that the faithful may request the *vitandi* and the *tolerati post sententiam* to administer the other sacraments (besides Penance) and sacramentals only in danger of death when no other ministers are present. In the case under consideration, there is no question of danger of death, hence Canon 2261, § 3 cannot be invoked. Furthermore, there is no notable spiritual necessity or utility that would justify assistance at marriage on the part of such priests.[71]

70 Can. 2261, § 3. Cf. Cerato, *Matrimonium a Codice Juris Canonici integre Desumptum,* n. 98; Leitner, *Lehrbuch des katholischen Eherechts,* p. 207.

71 Cf. can. 1095, § 1, n. 1.

The priest who assists at a marriage in virtue of Canon 1098, n. 2, is granted certain powers of dispensing. Thus, in (urgent) danger of death, and for cases in which the local Ordinary cannot be approached, for the sake of conscience, and, if the case warrants it, for the legitimation of offspring, he can dispense from the prescribed form and also from all impediments of ecclesiastical law, whether they are public or occult, even if they are multiple, with the exception of the impediment arising from Sacred Priesthood and the impediment arising from affinity in the direct line, when the marriage has been consummated; scandal must be removed; if a dispensation is granted from the impediment of disparity of cult or of mixed religion, the customary promises are to be given.[72] Furthermore, whenever an impediment is discovered only after everything has been prepared for the marriage, and the marriage cannot be delayed without danger of grave evil, he can dispense from all the above-mentioned impediments, but only for occult cases, that is, impediments *de facto* occult, whatever their nature may be,[73] in which the local Ordinary cannot be approached, or only with danger of violating the secret.[74] Under the same circumstances, this faculty avails for the convalidation of a marriage already contracted.[75]

To grant a dispensation is an exercise of the power of jurisdiction. According to Canon 2264, the *vitandi* and the *tolerati post sententiam* cannot validly exercise the power of jurisdiction either of the internal or of the external forum. Some exceptions to this law have already been seen.[76] The question now arises whether a *vitandus* or a *toleratus post sententiam*, as the priest who assists at marriage in virtue of Canon 1098, n. 2, can make use of the faculty of dispensing granted such a priest by Canons 1044 and 1045, § 3.

72 Can. 1044.
73 Pont. Comm., Feb. 1, 1928, (*AAS*, XX, p. 61).
74 Can. 1045, § 3.
75 Can. 1045, § 2.
76 *Supra*, p. 95, p. 106.

It seems certain that when one of the parties is in danger of death, even the *vitandi* and the *tolerati post sententiam* can make use of the faculty of dispensing granted by Canon 1044. Canon 2261, § 3 states that the faithful when in danger of death may petition the *vitandi* and the *tolerati post sententiam* to administer the other sacraments (besides Penance) and sacramentals, if no other ministers are present. True it is, in the cases which come under Canon 1098, abstracting, of course, from the presence of impediments in the cases, the presence of a priest is not required for the valid reception of the Sacrament of Matrimony; the contracting parties themselves are the ministers of the Sacrament; furthermore, the sacramentals which have place in the Catholic form of marriage are by no means necessity for the validity of the Sacrament. However, to ask a *vitandus* or a *toleratus post sententiam* to dispense from an impediment is equivalent to petitioning the administration of a sacrament, since the sacrament cannot be received, unless the impediment is removed. Hence, it seems that a *vitandus* or a *toleratus post sententiam,* who, in virtue of Canon 1098, n. 2, assists at the marriage of a person in danger of death, can make use of the faculty of dispensing granted by Canon 1044.

The question, however, presents some difficulties with regard to the other case that comes under Canon 1098, that is, when it is prudently foreseen that a competent priest will not be available for a month and the circumstances mentioned in Canon 1045, § 1 are verified. There is no question of danger of death, consequently Canon 2261, § 3 cannot be invoked, as it was in the preceding paragraph. Hence it would seem that the *vitandi* and the *tolerati post sententiam* cannot make use of the faculty of dispensing granted by Canon 1045, § 3. Canon 2264, which treats of the exercise of the power of jurisdiction by excommunicates, makes exception with regard to the *vitandi* and the *tolerati post sententiam* only for the cases which come under Canon 2261, § 3.

CHAPTER IV

INDULGENCES, SUFFRAGES, PUBLIC PRAYERS

CANON 2262

§ 1. Excommunicatus non fit particeps indulgentiarum, suffragiorum, publicarum Ecclesiae precum.

§ 2. Non prohibentur tamen:

1.° Fideles privatim pro eo orare;

2.° Sacerdotes Missam privatim ac remoto scandalo pro eo applicare; sed, si sit vitandus, pro ejus conversione tantum.

Pre-Code authors spoke of the effect of excommunication which we are about to consider as *privatio communium Ecclesiae suffragiorum.*[1] "The technical term for this effect of excommunication is '*privatio communium Ecclesiae suffragiorum,*' viz.: privation of the spiritual aids by which members of the Church assist one another in order either to atone for temporal punishments (*per satisfactionem*) or to obtain, either directly or indirectly, spiritual benefits (*per impetrationem*)."[2]

Suffrages may be either private or common. Private suffrages are those which are offered by the faithful in their own name; they embrace prayers, fastings, alms and other good works which are performed by the faithful in their own name, or by the ministers of the Church in their own name and as private persons.[3] As we shall

---

1 Schmalzgrueber, pars IV, tit. XXXIX, n. 126; Reiffenstuel, lib. V, tit. XXXIX, n. 57; Wernz, VI, n. 188.

2 Augustine, *Commentary,* VIII, p. 184.

3 Cf. Sole, *De Delictis et Poenis,* n. 222; Augustine, *Commentary,* VIII, p. 184.

see more fully later, excommunicates are not deprived of a participation in private suffrages.

Common suffrages, of which alone excommunicates are deprived, are those which are offered in the name of the Church and "quae ex sacrificio Missae totius Ecclesiae nomine oblato, ex publicis ministrorum officiis et orationibus, ex publico et communi thesauro satisfactionum Ecclesiae per indulgentias Praelatorum auctoritate applicatas fidelibus provenire solent."[4]

It is clear from what has been said that the word *suffragia* was employed as a generic term to designate all the spiritual aids which accrued to the faithful from the treasury of the Church and from the prayers, good works, etc., offered in the name of the Church. Canon 2262, § 1, however, speaks separately of indulgences, suffrages and public prayers of the Church. The distinction which exists between indulgences and the other spiritual fruits derived by the faithful from the supplications of the Church is readily seen. An indulgence is a remission before God of the temporal punishment due for sins already forgiven which the ecclesiastical authority grants from the treasury of the Church to the living *per modum absolutionis* and to the departed *per modum suffragii.*[5]

Canon 2262, § 1, seems to imply that there is a distinction between suffrages and public prayers of the Church. Just in what this distinction consists is difficult to say. Some canonists have made a noble effort to show forth the distinction, but it would seem that they have not succeeded in clarifying matters. For the most part, they seem to speak of practically the same thing, first, under the name *suffragia*, and then under the title *publicae Ecclesiae preces.*

4 Wernz, VI, n. 188; cf. Schmalzgrueber, pars IV, tit. XXXIX, n. 126; Reiffenstuel, lib. V, tit. XXXIX, n. 57; Sole, *De Delictis et Poenis*, n. 222; Vermeersch-Creusen, *Epitome*, III, n. 464.

5 Can. 911.

Cappello[6] and Augustine[7] consider suffrages as having special reference to the fruits of the Mass, in so far, as Cappello very well remarks, as the celebration of Mass is an action of the Church. Cerato[8] and Sole[9] look upon public prayers of the Church as those which are performed liturgically by sacred ministers in the name of the Church, "sive in ecclesia, sive extra ecclesiam, cum populo vel sine eo."

Perhaps Augustine is nearer the correct solution than any of the authors when he says that suffrages have reference especially to the fruits of the Mass, and to prayers and good works, such as alms and penances which are offered *by way of satisfaction*, and that the public prayers of the Church may be understood as prayers chiefly, though not exclusively, *of impetratory intercession* offered in the name of the Church.[10]

Prescinding from indulgences, it may be said in general that suffrages and the public prayers of the Church include within their scope all the supplications, good works, etc., of either satisfactory or impetratory merit, which are offered in the name of the Church.

Pre-Code authors were unanimous in maintaining that the *vitandi* were excluded from a participation in the common suffrages of the Church. This exclusion was of such a nature that although a minister of the Church wished to apply indulgences to them, or to offer for them public prayers, or to apply to them the fruits of the Mass, in so far as they are in the power of the Church, the applications were of no value, just as the distribution of the master's money by a servant is of no value, if made against the will of the Master.[11] Some were of the opinion that the common suffrages could be offered for a *vitandus* who was contrite and had recovered the state

---

6 *De Censuris*, n. 156.
7 *Commentary, VIII*, p. 184.
8 *Censurae Vigentes*, n. 37.
9 *De Delictis et Poenis*, n. 222.
10 *Commentary*, VIII, p. 184. (The italics are the writer's.)
11 Schmalzgrueber, pars IV, tit. XXXIX, n. 126; Ballerini-Palmieri, *Opus Theologicum Morale*, VII, n. 386.

of sanctifying grace.[12] Saint Alphonsus, however, characterized the negative view-point as *longe probabilior.*[13] It was disputed among pre-Code authors whether the common suffrages could be applied to the *tolerati.* Saint Alphonsus considered both the affirmative and the negative opinions as probable.[14] The former opinion was based on the Constitution "*Ad vitanda*" which permitted the faithful to communicate *in divinis* as well as *in humanis* with the *tolerati.* Furthermore, the defenders of this opinion argued, formerly it was not forbidden to offer public suffrages for occult excommunicates.[15] The defenders of the negative opinion responded that the Constitution "*Ad vitanda*" was by no means meant to better the condition of the *tolerati,* and that it gave leave to the faithful to communicate only externally with the *tolerati.*[16] Wernz, however, narrows down the *tolerati* who were excluded from the common suffrages to those whose excommunication was publicly known.[17]

The Code has put an end to the discussion. Without making any distinction between the *vitandi* and the *tolerati,* Canon 2262, § 1, states that an excommunicate has no share in the indulgences, suffrages and public prayers of the Church. Indulgences, suffrages and public prayers of the Church are within the power of the Church and hence, their concession and dispensation is dependent upon the will of the Church. The reason for this exclusion is evident from the very nature of the censure of excommunication. Excommunication places one outside the communion of the faithful, and consequently, deprives one of participation in all the benefits which accrue to the faithful by reason of this communion.[18] This exclusion is such that no private application of the *suffrages* and *public prayers* of the Church is of any

---

12 Cf. apud Suarez, *De Censuris,* disp. IX, s. 3, n. 1.
13 *Theologia Moralis,* VII, n. 163; cf. c. 28, X, *de sent. excom.* V. 39.
14 *Theologia Moralis,* VII, n. 164.
15 C. 14, X, *de sent. excom.* V, 30; cf. S. Alphonsus, *Theologia Moralis,* VII, n. 164.
16 Suarez, *De Censuris,* disp. IX, s. 3, n. 2; Wernz, VI, n. 188.
17 *Loc. cit.*
18 Cf. Sole, *De Delictis et Poenis,* n. 222.

avail. No one, of course, can apply an indulgence to another living person.[19]

The question now arises whether indulgences can be applied to those who died while under ban of excommunication and who have not been absolved from the censure after death. D'Annibale,[20] Cerato,[21] Chelodi,[22] and Pighi,[23] are of the opinion that even the departed excommunicates are deprived of a participation in indulgences.

A censure is not removed except by legitimate absolution and generally as long as a censure remains it has its effects. There is no doubt but that the Church could remove the privation of indulgences, suffrages and public prayers of the Church in the case of departed excommunicates. There seems to be no juridical basis, however, for maintaining that the Church has done so. Innocent III declared that an excommunicate who died before being absolved from the censure, even though before death he gave manifest signs of repentance and there was nothing to prevent his reconciliation with the Church, was not absolved in the eyes of the Church, and that he must be absolved after death. This was a response given to the question "Utrum pro tali recipienda sit eleemosyna et a fidelibus sit orandum."[24] In another canon found in the Decretals of Gregory IX, the same Pontiff (Innocent III) declared that for a departed person who had incurred excommunication by communicating with an excommunicate "nec * * * oblationes recipiendae pro eo, vel orationes Domino porrigendae, nisi quum de ipsius viventis poenitentia per evidentia signa constiterit, et juxta cujusdam constitutionis nostrae tenorem defuncto etiam absolutionis beneficium impendatur."[25] Furthermore, the Roman ritual, in the rubrics preceding the rite of absolving a departed

19 Can. 930.

20 *Summula Theologia Moralis*, I, n. 360, not. 8.

21 *Censurae Vigentes*, n. 37.

22 *Jus Poenale*, n. 37.

23 *Censurae Sententiae Latae*, n. 21.

24 C. 28, X, *de sent. excom.* V, 39.

25 C. 38, X, *de sent. excom.* V, 39.

excommunicate, states that if an excommunicate gave sign of contrition before death, he can be absolved "ne ecclesiastica careat sepultura sed Ecclesiae suffragiis, quatenus fieri potest, adjuvetur."[26]

Hence, it would seem that, as far as the Church is concerned, the effect of excommunication by which those under its ban are deprived of a participation in indulgences, suffrages and public prayers of the Church is not removed with regard to deceased excommunicates, that is, those who even after death have not been absolved from the censure.

Cappello, however, asserts that the opinion which denies to departed excommunicates a participation in indulgences is not certain, and does not seem to be the truer one, since indulgences are granted to the deceased *per modum suffragii*.[27]

Apropos of this discussion, it may be well to make a few remarks of practical value. Whenever possible, according to the teaching of Moral Theology and the norm laid down in the Ritual, an excommunicate who died before being reconciled with the Church should be absolved from the censure after death. The fact that an excommunicate cannot be granted the benefit of absolution after death is no reason why the faithful should neglect to pray for the repose of his soul.

Non prohibentur tamen fideles privatim pro eo orare.

The faithful are not forbidden to pray privately for excommunicates whether they are *vitandi* or *tolerati*. Although excommunicates do not communicate with God through the mediumship of the Church, yet communication with God, in so far as it can exist without the Church, is still possible for them. For this reason they are not deprived of the private suffrages and prayers of the faithful. Just as excommunicates can pray for themselves, so others can storm heaven with prayers in their behalf. Moreover, to pray for excommunicated persons

26 Tit. III, cap. 4.
27 *De Censuris*, n. 156.

is truly a work of mercy, just as it is a work of mercy to pray for infidels that they receive the light of faith and for sinners that they be converted from their evil ways.[28] The faithful may pray privately for any legitimate intention of an excommunicate.

The faithful may pray only privately (*privatim*) for excommunicates. Hence, they are forbidden implicitly to pray publicly for them. It may be said that prayers are offered privately, not only when they are offered in secret by one individual, but also when they are offered by a number in a private place. On the contrary, prayers are said to be public, when they are offered by many in a public manner and in a public place, ex. gr., in a Church, even though no sacred minister participates in them.[29]

Non prohibentur tamen sacerdotes Missam privatim ac remoto scandalo pro eo applicare; sed, si sit vitandus, pro ejus conversione tantum.

There was much controversy among pre-Code authors concerning the application of Mass for excommunicates.[30] Some maintained that it was forbidden to apply Mass even privately and secretly for all excommunicates.[31] After the publication of the Constitution "*Ad vitanda*" some authors were of the opinion that Mass could be applied secretly for the *tolerati* and that Mass could be offered for the *vitandi,* not in the name of the Church, but in the name of the celebrant.[32] Scarcely anyone denied that a priest could remember even the *vitandi* in the Memento of the Mass, just as he could offer other private supplications for them; likewise, he could offer Mass indirectly for their conversion, by applying it, ex. gr., for the exaltation of the Church, for the conversion of sinners.[33] Gasparri sponsored substantially

---

28 Cf. Sole, *De Delictis et Poenis,* n. 223.
29 Cerato, *Censurae Vigentes,* n. 37. Cf. Blat, *De Delictis et Poenis,* n. 89.
30 Cf. Gasparri, *De Eucharistia,* I, n. 483.
31 Cf. Salmanticences, Tract. V, *De Sacrif. Missae,* Cap. II, p. II, n. 16.
32 S. Alphonsus, *Theologia Moralis,* VI, n. 309; de Lugo, *Tractatus de Eucharistia,* disp. XIX, s. X, n. 185.
33 Gasparri, *De Eucharistia,* I, n. 483.

the same solution of the problem as is found in the Code.[34]

Before commenting upon the portion of Canon 2262 that is now under discussion, it might be well to say a few words about the fruits of the Mass. Three fruits of the Mass may be distinguished, namely; the most special or personal fruit, the special or ministerial fruit and the general fruit. The most special or personal fruit of the Mass is that which accrues to the worthy celebrant and which cannot be wholly applied to another. The special or ministerial fruit is that which benefits the person or end for which the Mass is offered. The general fruit of the Mass is that which benefits in the first place those that minister and assist at the Holy Sacrifice and in the second place all the faithful, both living and dead, as long as there is no obstacle to their participating in this benefit.[35]

Canon 2262, § 2, 2°, states that priests are not forbidden to apply Mass for excommunicates *privatim ac remoto scandalo;* but, if the excommunicate is a *vitandus,* Mass can be applied only for his conversion. The canon evidently has reference to *applying Mass* in the proper sense of the term, that is, offering Mass for a person or intention in such a manner that the person or intention will be benefited by the special or ministerial fruit of the Mass. Canon 809 employs the phrase *applicare Missam* and it is certain that this canon has reference to the application of the special or ministerial fruit of the Mass. Furthermore, Canon 2262 cannot have reference to the most special or personal fruit of the Mass, nor to the general fruit. If the former can be applied to another at all, there is no reason why it cannot be applied to any excommunicate. With regard to the general fruit of the Mass, excommunicates have no share in it.[36]

In other words, a priest may offer Mass for excommunicates and their intentions, just as for other persons.

---

34 *Op. et loc. cit.*

35 Genicot-Salsmans, *Institutiones Theologiae Moralis,* 10 ed., II, n. 217.

36 Can. 2262, § 1.

There are two restrictions, however. The first is that Mass must be applied *privatim ac remoto scandalo.* The second is that when the excommunicate is a *vitandus,* Mass can be offered only for his conversion. Thus the Church makes known what is most necessary and what should be the first concern of the *vitandi.*[37] Since there is question here of applying the ministerial fruits of the Mass, priests may accept stipends for the Masses which are offered for excommunicates and their intentions.[38]

The Mass must be applied *privatim ac remoto scandalo.* Primarily, it is the application of the Mass, that is, the intention for which the Mass is offered and not the Mass itself, or the celebration thereof, that must be private. Private application of Mass is opposed to a public application thereof. Hence, the fact that Mass is to be offered for an excommunicate or his intention cannot be made public. No announcement to this effect can be made from the pulpit, or in a parish publication, or in any other manner.

Many writers are of the opinion that the Mass which is applied for an excommunicate or his intention cannot be a Solemn Mass, or a *Missa cantata,* but must be a private or low Mass.[39] However, according to the canon, it is the application of the Mass, that is, the intention for which the Mass is offered, that must be private. It is not necessary that the Mass itself be a private one, that is, a *Missa privata.* It must be admitted, however, that the opinion of Cerato, Augustine, etc., is in strict accord with the spirit of the Church in dealing in these matters with her recalcitrant children. Hence, ordinarily, a priest must refuse to celebrate other than a private or low Mass for an excommunicate; to act otherwise would very often give rise to scandal. There are some cases, however, in which a priest would be fully justified in applying a Solemn Mass or a *Missa cantata* for an excommunicate.

---

37 Cerato, *Censurae Vigentes,* n. 37.

38 Cf. *S. C. S. O.,* April 19, 1837, (*Fontes,* n. 876); July 12, 1865, (*Fontes,* n. 985).

39 Ex. gr., Cerato, *Censurae Vigentes,* n. 37; Augustine, *Commentary,* VIII, p. 185.

Take the case in which a priest is requested to offer Mass for an excommunicate and the time of the Mass is left at the disposal of the priest. There seems to be no reason why the priest may not apply for the excommunicate a Solemn Mass or a *Missa cantata* which he is obliged to sing by reason of his parish duties. In the case, the application of the Mass is private; furthermore, no scandal results from such a course of action, for, as the case supposes, not even the donor of the stipend is aware when the Mass is to be offered.

In all cases in which Mass is offered for an excommunicate, scandal must be avoided. For the most part, the law itself has taken care that no scandal will arise by stating that the application of the Mass must be private. Hence, ordinarily the only ones who might be scandalized by such a course of action are those who petition the Mass. This would very seldom be the case. However, any danger of scandal can easily be removed by a prudent explanation of the Church's legislation in this matter and the reason thereof.

It remains to say a few words concerning the application of Mass for deceased excommunicates. Mass may be applied, even publicly, for any excommunicate who was admitted to ecclesiastical burial.[40] Hence, Mass may be offered, even publicly, for the repose of the soul of a *vitandus* or a *toleratus post sententiam* who manifested signs of repentance before death, and likewise, for the repose of the soul of a *simpliciter toleratus* who departed without giving signs of repentance, for such excommunicates are not to be deprived Christian burial.[41] May Mass be applied for a departed *vitandus* or *toleratus post sententiam* who died without manifesting any signs of repentance and who consequently was denied ecclesiastical sepulture? It would seem that Mass may be offered (*privatim ac remoto scandalo*) for such a *toleratus*,[42] unless it is *certain* that he was in bad faith and died impeni-

40 Cf. Cappello, *De Censuris*, n. 156.
41 Cf. Can. 1240, § 1, n. 2.
42 Cf. Cappello, *De Sacramentis*, I, n. 621.

tent. With regard to a *vitandus,* the question is rather difficult. Augustine remarks: "It is a rather venturesome interpretation to allow Mass to be said for a dead *vitandus,* i. e., one who died under such an excommunication, because the text allows it to be done only for his conversion, which after death is impossible."[43] Chelodi is of the opinion that Mass cannot be offered for a deceased *vitandus.*[44] Pighi asserts that Mass cannot be offered for such a one, at least publicly.[45] It is to be noted, however, that the canon under discussion does not explicitly forbid the application of Mass for a deceased *vitandus.* In fact, it makes no direct reference whatsoever to departed excommunicates. True it is, it states that Mass can be applied only for the conversion of a *vitandus* and after death there is no possibility of conversion. Yet, since the Church permits Mass to be offered for what is best for a *vitandus* in life, that is, his conversion, does it not seem unreasonable to claim that the Church forbids the application of Mass for a deceased *vitandus?* To interpret Canon 2262, § 2, n. 2, as forbidding the application of Mass for a deceased *vitandus* seems to be contrary to the rules governing penal interpretation. Since the canon speaks of applying Mass only for the conversion of a *vitandus,* a strict interpretation would lead to the conclusion that the legislator has taken into consideration only the question of applying Mass for the living *vitandus.* This conclusion would be reached by the same reason which the upholders of the negative view-point give for their opinion, namely, that after death there is no possibility of conversion. Hence, the opinion may be ventured that Mass may be offered *privatim ac remoto scandalo* for a deceased *vitandus,* unless it is *certain* that he was in bad faith and died unrepentent.[46]

---

43 *Commentary,* VIII, n. 186-187.
44 *Jus Poenale,* n. 37.
45 *Censurae Sententiae Latae,* n. 21.
46 Cf. Wernz, VI, n. 188; Gasparri, *De Eucharistia,* n. 483; Ayrinhac, *Penal Legislation,* p. 124.

CHAPTER V

Legitimate Ecclesiastical Acts: Excommunicates as Plaintiffs in Ecclesiastical Courts: Discharge of Ecclesiastical Offices: Use of Privileges

CANON 2263

Removetur excommunicatus ab actibus legitimis ecclesiasticis intra fines suis in locis jure definitos; nequit in causis ecclesiasticis agere, nisi ad norman can. 1654; prohibetur ecclesiasticis officiis seu muneribus fungi, concessisque antea ab Ecclesia privilegiis frui.

I. Legitimate Ecclesiastical Acts

Removetur excommunicatus ab actibus legitimis ecclesiasticis intra fines suis in locis jure definitos.

The Code is quite in conformity with the old law in removing excommunicates from what are now known as legitimate ecclesiastical acts.[1] Prior to the Code, this effect of excommunication was not found stated in any one canon or decree. It was scattered throughout the *Corpus Juris Canonici.* True it is, in the Decretals of Boniface VIII, there is a reference to the removal of public excommunicates from legitimate acts. It is very difficult, however, to ascertain just what were included within the scope of legitimate acts, for in the very same sentence, the canon speaks of avoiding public excommunicates not only in judicial but also in extrajudicial affairs.[2]

1 Blat, *Commentarium,* V, *De Delictis et Poenis,* n. 90.

2 " * * * et nedum in judicialibus, sed etiam in extrajudicialibus evitari, ac a legitimis actibus removeri debebit." C. 14, *de sent. excom.* V, 11 in VI.

The Code gives a taxative enumeration of what are now to be understood as legitimate ecclesiastical acts. By the term *legitimate ecclesiastical acts* are understood: the office of administrator of ecclesiastical goods; the functions of those persons in ecclesiastical causes who act as judge, auditor and relator, *defensor vinculi,* promoter of justice and of faith, notary and chancellor, *cursor* and *apparitor,* advocate and procurator; the office of sponsor in the Sacraments of Baptism and Confirmation; voting in ecclesiastical elections; exercising the *juspatronatus.*[3]

Pre-Code Discipline

Administrator of Ecclesiastical Goods. There seems to have been no explicit and direct legislation removing excommunicates from the office of administrator of ecclesiastical goods. However, authors deduced such an exclusion from the very nature and notion of excommunication.[4]

Judicial Procedure. Under the law of the Decretals, excommunicates were deprived of all forensic communication. They could not act the part of judge, arbiter, advocate, procurator, witness, notary, secretary, etc.[5] At first this exclusion extended to all excommunicates whose censure was publicly known. After the Constitution "*Ad vitanda,*" it was applied in its full rigor only to the *vitandi,* who could not *validly* exercise any act pertaining to ecclesiastical courts. They were to be excluded absolutely and *ex officio,* whether the faithful or the interested parties demanded it or not. The *tolerati* could not *licitly* exercise any act pertaining to ecclesiastical

[3] Can. 2256, n. 2.

[4] "* * * de qua re nihil invenio expresse et in particulari in jure definitum. Est nihilominus illa sententia vera ex generali ratione, et privatione communicationis, quam affert excommunicatio major." Suarez, *De Censuris,* disp. XIII, s. 2, n. 6. Cf. Crnica, *Modificationes in Tractatu de Censuris,* p. 101.

[5] C. 24, 26, C. II, q. 7; c. 4, C. XXIV, q. 1; c. 39, X, *de sent. excom.* V, 39; c. 24, X, *de sent. et re jud.* II, 27; c. 1, *de sent. et re jud.* II, 14 in VI°; c. 13, § 5, X, *de haeret.* V, 7; c. 8, *de sent. excom.* V. 11 in VI°; c. 7, X, *de jud.* II, 1; c. 7, X, *de prob.* II, 19; c. 7, X, *de except.* II, 25; c. 1, X, *de haeret.* V, 7.

courts, unless they were requested to do so. Their exercise of judicial acts, however, was always valid, unless the exception of excommunication was opposed to them by the judge *ex officio,* or by one of the interested parties. Since the faithful had the option of associating with the *tolerati* or not, they could object to their being admitted to judicial procedure in any capacity. Since it often happened that the exception of excommunication was made maliciously and solely for the purpose of delaying the case, it was enacted that the excommunication of the person to whom exception was taken had to be proven within eight days.[6] When the censure was proven, the person had to be removed from the procedure.

This effect of excommunication at one time extended to the exercise of judicial acts even in secular courts, and to at least the licit acquisition of public civil offices.[7] This may seem rather strange at the present time, but it must be remembered that at one time the State recognized the effects of excommunication and aided the Church to enforce them. Long before the promulgation of the Code, this portion of the law fell into desuetude.

Sponsorship at Baptism and Confirmation. Because of the grave duties which the sponsors at Baptism and Confirmation assume, the Church has always been solicitous that no one be admitted in this capacity whose mode of living did not guarantee the fulfillment of the sponsorial duties. Consequently, public sinners and those who were publicly known to be under ban of excommunication have always been excluded from acting in this capacity. The Roman Ritual stated explicitly that public excommunicates were not to be admitted as Baptismal sponsors.[8] Explicit reference is made to the exclusion of excommunicates from sponsorship at Confirmation in the Roman Pontifical,[9] and in an instruction

6 C. 1, *de except.* II, 12 in VI°.

7 Schmalzgrueber, pars. IV, tit, XXXIX, n. 170; Suarez, *De Censuris,* disp, VII, s. 1, n. 1; Wernz, VI, n. 195; cf. c. 13, X, *de poenis,* V, 37.

8 Tit. II, cap. 1, nn. 22-26.

9 Tit. *De Confirmandis.*

of the Sacred Congregation for the Propogation of the Faith, issued on May 4, 1774.[10]

Voting in Canonical Elections. The *vitandi* could not validly take part in canonical elections. Votes cast by the *tolerati,* however, were valid, unless exception was taken to their participating in the election.[11]

The Exercise of the Juspatronatus. The exercise of the *juspatronatus* was forbidden to all under ban of major excommunication. Hence, presentation by an excommunicate was always illicit; if the excommunicate was a *vitandus,* the presentation was invalid and could not be admitted by the superior; if the excommunicate was a *toleratus,* the superior could admit the presentation, but was not obliged to do so.[12]

The Present Discipline

Canon 2263 states that an excommunicate is removed from legitimate ecclesiastical acts within the limits specified in the various places in law. What is the meaning of the clause "intra fines suis in locis jure definitos"? A strict interpretation of this clause would lead to the conclusion that excommunicates are removed from legitimate ecclesiastical acts only in so far as their removal therefrom is stated in the canons which treat specifically of the various legitimate ecclesiastical acts. A few examples may help to clarify this statement. Sponsorship at baptism is a legitimate ecclesiastical act. According to Canon 765, n. 2, the *vitandi* and the *tolerati* against whom a declaratory or condemnatory sentence has been passed cannot validly act as sponsors, and according to Canon 766, n. 2, persons who are excommunicated for some notorious delict cannot licitly be admitted in this capacity. No mention is made in these canons of other excommunicates. Hence, according to the interpretation given above, all other excommunicates may freely and of

---

10 *Coll. S. C. P. F.*, n. 503.

11 Wernz, II, n. 357, not. 29; cf. c. 23, X, *de appell.* II, 28; c. unic. *ne sede vac.* III, 8 in VI°.

12 Wernz, II, n. 440; cf. Suarez, *De Censuris*, disp. XIV, s. 2, n. 30ss.

their own accord offer themselves to act as sponsors. In other words, all other excommunicates are *permitted* to act in the capacity of baptismal sponsor. In the section of the Code which treats of the administration of ecclesiastical goods,[13] another legitimate ecclesiastical act, no mention is made of excommunicates acting as administrators.[14] Hence, according to the interpretation given above, no excommunicate is forbidden to act in this capacity. These are some of the results of a strict interpretation of the clause "intra fines suis in locis jure definitos," and, according to general principles, a strict interpretation should be followed in this matter. Blat seems to follow the strict interpretation, for commenting upon the clause under discussion, he writes "ultra quos non extendatur remotio."[15]

The following interpretation is proposed as more in conformity with the nature of excommunication and with the other effects of the censure.

It would seem that no excommunicate may licitly exercise any legitimate ecclesiastical act. This seems to be the opinion of Pighi,[16] Chelodi[17] and Cappello.[18] Chelodi, enumerating the essential effects of excommunication, writes: " * * * quilibet excommunicatus prohibetur * * * actus legitimos ponere * * *." Cappello, treating of the effects of excommunication which are common to all under ban of this censure, writes: "Excommunicatus nequit actus legitimos ponere * * * Actus legtimi ecclesiastici, ab excommunicato [tolerato] positi, sunt * * * illiciti * * *." That this opinion is correct seems evident from the other effects of excommunication. "Prohibetur [excommunicatus] ecclesiasticis officiis seu muneribus fungi."[19] The Code itself speaks of the office of administrator of ecclesiastical goods and of

13 Can. 1518-1528.

14 Cf. however, Canons 1520, § 1 and 1521, § 1, which speak of the qualities of those who are to be appointed as administrators.

15 *Commentarium*, V, *De Delictis et Poenis*, n. 90.

16 *Censurae Sententiae Latae*, n. 24.

17 *Jus Poenale*, n. 37.

18 *De Censuris*, n. 150.

19 Can. 2263.

sponsorship at Baptism and Confirmation as *munera.* Certainly most of the judicial offices listed among the legitimate ecclesiastical acts are, to say the very least, ecclesiastical *munera.* The offices of judge, auditor and relator require an exercise of the power of jurisdiction, and, according to Canon 2264, no excommunicate can licitly exercise that power. The exercise of the *juspatronatus* consists principally in the right of presentation, and, according to Canon 2265, § 1, n. 1, no excommunicate may licitly exercise this right.

The clause, "intra fines suis in locis jure definitos" seems to be a guide to determine whether the placing of a legitimate ecclesiastical act by an excommunicate is, besides being illicit, invalid as well. Furthermore, it is to be understood not only concerning the places in law which treat specifically of the legitimate ecclesiastical acts, but likewise with reference to the other canons dealing with the effects of excommunication.

Canon 2232, § 1 must be kept in mind when there is question of excommunicates' exercising legitimate ecclesiastical acts. As has already been seen, this canon states that a *latae sententiae* penalty, whether medicinal or vindictive, *ipso facto* binds the delinquent who is conscious of the delict in both forums; before a declaratory sentence, however, the delinquent is excused from observing the penalty whenever he cannot observe it without loss of good repute, and no one can exact the observance of the penalty in the external forum, unless the delict is notorious.

Administrator of Ecclesiastical Goods.

No excommunicate can licitly exercise the office of administrator of ecclesiastical goods, either as an individual or as a member of a board of administration. No excommunicate can licitly acquire such an office.[20] The acquisition of such an office, however, is not invalid, unless the excommunicate is a *vitandus* or a *toleratus* against whom a declaratory or condemnatory sentence

20 Can. 2265, § 1, n. 2.

has been passed.[21] It would seem that acts of administration of ecclesiastical goods are invalid only when posited by a *vitandus*. This follows from Canon 2266 by which a *vitandus* is *ipso facto* deprived of any *munus* which he may hold, and consequently of the office of administrator of ecclesiastical property, and likewise of any benefice or office to which the administration of church goods may be annexed. There seems to be no law which invalidates acts of administration of church property which are posited by the *tolerati post sententiam* who held such an office before the sentence was pronounced against him. This seems rather strange in view of the fact that the Code has practically placed the *tolerati post sententiam* in the same category as the *vitandi*, and generally attaches invalidly not only to acts placed by the *vitandi* but also to those posited by the *tolerati post sententiam*.[22]

Judicial Procedure.

According to the interpretation which has been given to Canon 2263, no excommunicate can licitly act as judge, auditor and relator, *defensor vinculi*, promoter of justice and of faith, notary and chancellor, *cursor* and *apparitor*, advocate and procurator in ecclesiastical causes. It is to be noted that an excommunicate is forbidden to act as judge, auditor and relator by virtue of Canon 2264, for these offices require an exercise of the power of jurisdiction.

It does not seem to be correct to cite Canon 1654, § 2 as permitting the *simpliciter tolerati* to hold office in ecclesiastical courts, unless they are repelled. This canon reads: "Alii excommunicati generatim stare in judicio queunt." It seems to have reference to admitting the *simpliciter tolerati* as plaintiffs and not in any other capacity. This seems clear from § 1 of the same canon, which mentions in what cases the *vitandi* and the *tolerati post sententiam* may be admitted as plaintiffs. Further-

21 Can. 2265, § 2.
22 Cf. Can. 2264; 2265, § 2.

more, Canon 1654 comes under the title, *"De Partibus in causa"* and under the caption, *"De actore et reo convento."*

The *simpliciter tolerati* always exercise the office of judge, auditor and relator, *defensor vinculi,* etc., validly. Moreover, they exercise them licitly, when they are requested either explicitly or implicitly by the faithful to do so; which, as Roberti very well remarks, is always the case in these matters.[23] It is clear from Canon 2264 that a *simpliciter toleratus* can licitly act as judge, or in any other capacity requiring an exercise of the power of jurisdiction, when requested to do so. It seems that the same is to be said of any other office in ecclesiastical courts, for this principle seems to run through this entire legislation.

Just as formerly, the faithful may object to the admission of the *simpliciter tolerati* to judicial procedure in any capacity. The exception of excommunication can be opposed in any stage or instance of the trial, up to the definitive sentence.[24] Noval is of the opinion that the exception of excommunication cannot be opposed in the appeal or in other remedies against the sentence.[25] Roberti takes exception to this opinion. He affirms that the exception of excommunication can be opposed in the appeal or in other remedies against the sentence. The definitive sentence, of which the canon speaks, is to be understood not only of the sentence of the first instance, but of the sentence of any instance ("in quolibet gradu"). "Dicitur 'definitiva' ut opponatur interlocutoriis."[26]

The *vitandi* and the *tolerati post sententiam* must always be excluded *ex officio* from any office in ecclesiastical courts.[27] They are to be excluded *ex officio,* that is, the judge is bound by reason of his office to exclude them, whether the interested parties demand it or not. It is to

---

23 *De Processibus,* I, n. 175.
24 Can. 1628, § 3.
25 *De Processibus,* pars I, *De Judiciis,* n. 222.
26 *De Processibus,* I, n. 175.
27 Can. 1628, § 3.

be noted that the *vitandi* and the *tolerati post sententiam* cannot validly act in the capacity of judge, auditor or relator, for these offices require an exercise of the power of jurisdiction.[28] Do such excommunicates invalidly exercise the office of notary, *defensor vinculi*, etc? Certainly, the *vitandi* cannot validly exercise such offices, for they are *ipso facto* deprived of any position which they hold in the Church.[29] The *tolerati post sententiam* could not validly exercise such offices, if they were appointed to them after the sentence had been passed against them.[30] There seems to be no law which *expressly* invalidates the exercise of such offices by the *tolerati post sententiam* who held such offices before the sentence was pronounced against them. Perhaps Canon 1628, § 3 does so *equivalently* when it states that such excommunicates "ex officio semper excludi debent." However, this discussion is of little practical import. It would not very often happen that a *vitandus* or a *toleratus post sententiam* would be admitted to an ecclesiastical trial in any official capacity.

It may be well to mention here in connection with judicial procedure, the legislation concerning excommunicates in the capacity of arbiters and witnesses, although neither acting as an arbiter, not testifying in ecclesiastical courts is listed among the legitimate ecclesiastical acts by Canon 2256, n. 2. The *vitandi* and the *tolerati post sententiam* cannot validly act in the capacity of arbiter.[31] The same classes of excommunicates are numbered among the *suspecti* who are repelled from testifying in ecclesiastical courts.[32] Their testimony, however, can be heard, if the judge deems it expedient, but it will avail only as an indication and support of the proof. Generally, they are to be heard without being placed under oath.[33]

---

28 Can. 2264; cf. Roberti, *De Processibus*, I, n. 110; Noval, *De Processibus*, pars I, *De Judiciis*, n. 131.

29 Can. 2266.

30 Can. 2265, § 2.

31 Can. 1931.

32 Can. 1757, § 2, n. 1.

33 Can. 1758.

Sponsorship at Baptism and Confirmation.

Since, practically speaking, the same qualifications are demanded of the sponsors at Confirmation as at Baptism, both shall be considered together. Hence, whenever mention is made of sponsors or sponsorship, reference is had both to the Sacrament of Baptism and to the Sacrament of Confirmation.

Canon 765 and 795 enumerate certain qualifications which are demanded for a valid sponsorship. This is evident from the very wording of the canons: "Ut quis sit patrinus." "The use of the word *esse* in this connection imports either existence or non-existence; hence, unless one be endowed with these essential qualifications for acting as sponsor, his actions would be considered null and void." [34] Furthermore, the conditions mentioned in Canons 766 and 796 are required in order that one can licitly be admitted as sponsor, which seems to imply that the qualifications demanded by the preceding canons are for validity.[35]

In order that one may validly act in the capacity of sponsor, it is required that he be not excommunicated by a condemnatory or declaratory sentence,[36] or, in other words, a *vitandus* or a *toleratus* against whom a condemnatory or declaratory sentence has been passed cannot validly act as sponsor. The qualifications which are demanded by Canons 765 and 795 must all be present in one and the same case to constitute a valid sponsorship. Hence, if a *vitandus* or a *toleratus post sententiam,* through forgetfulness, carelessness or disregard for the law of the Church was permitted to go through the formalities of a sponsor, his sponsorship would be invalid, even though he was endowed with all the other qualifications demanded by the canons; consequently, he would contract no spiritual relationship with the person baptized, nor would he be obliged to look after the spiritual welfare of the same.

---

34 Kearney, *Sponsors at Baptism,* p. 76.
35 *Ibidem.*
36 Can. 765, n. 2; 795, n. 2.

Canons 766 and 796 enumerate certain qualifications which are required in order that one may licitly be admitted as a sponsor. In order that one may licitly be admitted as sponsor, it is required, among other things, that he be not excommunicated for some notorious delict, or, in other words, a person who is excommunicated for some notorious delict cannot licitly be admitted as a sponsor.[87]

Canons 766 and 796 imply that occult excommunicates can licitly be *admitted* as sponsors. From this, however, one cannot conclude that such excommunicates can freely and of their own accord present themselves to act in the capacity of sponsor, or that such excommunicates are *simpliciter* permitted to act as sponsors. It is to be noted that Canons 766 and 796 do not treat precisely of those who can *licitly act* as sponsors, but of those who can *licitly be admitted* as sponsors: "Ut autem quis licite patrinus admittatur"; "Ut quis licite ad patrini munus admittatur." That the term *admittere* is to be understood in this sense seems clear from other portions of these canons in which reference is made to the judgment of the minister: "nisi aliud justa de causa ministro videatur"; "nisi rationabilis causa, judicio ministri, aliud suadeat"; "nisi aliud ministro in casibus particularibus ex rationabili causa videatur." Furthermore, Canon 766, n. 2 implies that one who is excluded from legitimate acts for a delict that is not notorious can licitly *be admitted* as sponsor. Certainly one who is excluded from legitimate acts, even for a delict that is not notorious, *per se* cannot licitly *act* as sponsor. The Code implies that persons who are excommunicated for a delict that is not notorious can licitly *be admitted* as sponsors. This is in conformity with Canon 2232 which states that before a declaratory sentence, no one can exact the observance of a *latae sententiae* penalty in the external forum, unless the delict is notorious. Hence, far from being at a variance with the interpretation that has been

87 Can. 766, n. 2; 796, n. 3.

given to Canon 2263, namely, that no excommunicate can licitly place any legitimate ecclesiastical act, Canons 766 and 796 seem to confirm it.

Voting in Ecclesiastical Elections.

No excommunicate can vote at least in those ecclesiastical elections which are conducted according to the regulations laid down in the Code under the caption "*De Electione.*"[38] Although these canons have reference primarily to election of a person to an ecclesiastical office in the strict sense of the term, yet the same regulations are followed whenever the votes of subjects designate a superior to rule a community, although without the power of jurisdiction in the strict sense of the term.[39] A vote cast by a *vitandus* or a *toleratus* against whom a declaratory or condemnatory sentence has been passed is invalid. The election itself, however, is not invalid, except in two cases: (1) when it is certain that the vote of the excommunicate was decisive, that is, when it is certain that without the vote of the excommunicate, the person elected would not have received a sufficient number of votes to gain the election; (2) when the excommunicate was knowingly (*scienter*) admitted to participate in the election.[40]

What has been said does not apply to the election of the Sovereign Pontiff which is governed by the Constitution "*Vacante Sede Apostolica,*" issued by Pope Pius X on December 25, 1904. It may be interesting to quote a portion of this Constitution which has some bearing upon the subject under discussion. "Nullus Cardinalium, cujuslibet excommunicationis, suspensionis, interdicti aut alius ecclesiastici impedimenti praetextu vel causa a Summi Pontificis electione activa et passiva excludi ullo modo potest; quas quidem censuras et excommunica-

---

38 Can. 160-178.

39 Vermeersch-Creusen, *Epitome,* I, n. 240; Can. 145, § 2; 507, § 1; cf. Maroto, *Institutiones Juris Canonici,* I, n. 611; Cocchi, *Commentarium,* II, n. 74.

40 Can. 167, § 2.

tiones ad effectum hujusmodi electionis tantum, illis alias in suo robore permansuris, suspendimus."[41]

The Right of Patronage.

The right of patronage is defined as the "summa privilegiorum, cum quibusdam oneribus, quae ex Ecclesiae concessione competunt fundatoribus catholicis ecclesiae, cappellae aut beneficii, vel etiam eis qui ab illis causam habent."[42]

The right of patronage may be either *real* or *personal.* It is *real* when it is attached to a thing; it is *personal* when it inheres in a person.[43]

Patrons have the privilege: 1) of presenting a cleric to a vacant church or benefice; 2) under certain circumstances and conditions of obtaining support from the revenue of the church or benefice; 3) of enjoying, where such is customary, certain prerogatives of honor, ex gr., of having their coat-of-arms placed in the church of their patronage, of preceding other laics in processions and similar functions, of having a more prominent seat in the church.[44]

A personal right of patronage cannot validly be transferred to the *vitandi* or the *tolerati* against whom a declaratory or condemnatory sentence has been pronounced.[45] If a thing to which a real right of patronage is attached passes into the possession of a *vitandus* or a *toleratus post sententiam,* the right of patronage remains suspended.[46] No excommunicated patron can licitly exercise the right of presentation,[47] nor enjoy the privileges which are attached to the right of patronage.[48] Presentation made by an excommunicated patron is not invalid, unless the patron is a *vitandus* or a *toleratus*

41 Tit. II, cap. I, n. 29, (*Codex Juris Canonici, Docum.* I). Cf. Motu Proprio Pii XI, "*Cum Proxime,*" (*AAS,* XIV, pp. 145-146).

42 Can. 1448.

43 Can. 1449, n. 1.

44 Can. 1455.

45 Can. 1453, § 1.

46 Can. 1453, § 3.

47 Can. 2265, § 1, n. 1.

48 Can. 2263.

against whom a declaratory or condemnatory sentence has been issued.[49] It would seem, too, that such excommunicates cannot validly make use of the privileges which accompany the right of patronage.[50]

II. Excommunicates as Plaintiffs in Ecclesiastical Courts

Nequit in causis ecclesiasticis agere, nisi ad normam can. 1654.

Canon 1654.

§ *1. Excommunicatis vitandis aut toleratis post sententiam declaratoriam vel condemnatoriam permittitur ut per se ipsi agant tantummodo ad impugnandam justitiam aut legitimitatem ipsius excommunicationis; per procuratorem, ad aliud quodvis animae suae praejudicium avertendum; in reliquis ab agendo repelluntur.*

§ *2. Alii excommunicati generatim stare in judicio queunt.*

Pre-Code Law

The general rule was that excommunicates could not be plaintiffs (*actores*) in ecclesiastical courts.[51] This prohibition, however, was applied in its full rigor only to the *vitandi*. With but few exceptions, they could not be plaintiffs, either personally or by proxy. Even though the exception of excommunication was not opposed to them by the interested parties, the judge was bound by reason of his office to repel them. The *vitandi*

---

49 Can. 2265, § 2; 1470, § 4.

50 Can. 1470, § 4.

51 C. 1, C. IV, q. 1; c. 4, C. VI, q. 1; c. 15, X, *de procuratoribus*, I, 38; c. 7, X, *de judiciis*, II, 1; c. 2, 5, 8, 11, 12, X, *de exceptionibus*, II, 25; c. 20, X, *de accusationibus, inquisitionibus et denuntiationibus*, V, 1; c. 1, *de exceptionibus* II, 12 in VI°; c. unic. *de exceptionibus*, II, 10 in Clem.

were admitted as plaintiffs in order to prove the invalidity of the sentence of excommunication. If, however, they desired to prove that it was unjust, they had to be absolved beforehand, since in this case, they seemed to admit that they were under ban of excommunication.[52] They were likewise admitted as plaintiffs in certain grave cases, especially when there was question of danger to soul, ex. gr., in matrimonial cases.[53]

Both the judge, by reason of his office, and the interested parties could oppose the exception of excommunication against a plaintiff who was a *toleratus,* but neither was obliged to do so.

This effect of excommunication once extended to secular courts. Thus Pope Alexander IV ordered secular judges to repel excommunicates from acting in their courts.[54] Long before the promulgation of the Code, however, this effect of excommunication, in so far as it extended to secular courts, had fallen into desuetude.

Excommunicates were obliged, when cited, to appear before an ecclesiastical court as defendant or accused. Otherwise they would be able to evade justice, avoid punishment and thus be aided rather than impeded by the censure.[55] The law expressly granted them full right of defending themselves.[56] At one time they were obliged to employ a procurator to defend them.[57] This obligation, however, was very seldom enforced, lest it seem as a denial of the right of self-defence, and gradually it fell into oblivion.[58]

The Present Law

The general principle is that anyone can be a plaintiff before an ecclesiastical court, unless he is prohibited

---

52 C. 40, X, *de sententia excommunicationis,* V, 39.

53 Cf. Wernz, V, n. 168, not. 64.

54 C. 8, *de sententia excommunicationis,* V, 11 in VI°.

55 Smith, *Elements of Ecclesiastical Law,* III, n. 3227.

56 C. 5, X, *de exceptionibus,* II, 25.

57 C. 7, X, *de judiciis,* II, 1.

58 Roberti, *De Processibus,* I, n. 205.

from doing so by the sacred canons.[59] Canon 2263 states that an excommunicate cannot be a plaintiff in ecclesiastical courts, except in so far as Canon 1654 permits. Before proceeding to discuss Canon 1654, it is well to point out that at the present time, this effect of excommunication extends only to ecclesiastical courts. The Code has not reënacted the law which once extended this prohibition even to secular courts. Of course, the faithful must avoid communication *in profanis* with the *vitandi,* unless there is question of husband or wife, parents, children, servants, subjects, or in general unless a reasonable cause excuses.[60]

Canon 1654, § 1 states that *vitandi* and the *tolerati* against whom a declaratory or condemnatory sentence has been issued can personally (*per se*) appear in court as plaintiffs, only when they desire to impugn the justice or the legitimacy (validity) of their excommunication. It is to be noted that the Code is more lenient in this regard than the former discipline, which, as has been seen, demanded the *vitandi* to be absolved before instituting an action against the justice of their excommunication. Canon 1654, § 1, further states that the *vitandi* and the *tolerati post sententiam* can be plaintiffs, but only by proxy, in order to avert any other spiritual danger. Authors generally cite matrimonial cases as examples of cases in which there is question of averting a spiritual danger.[61] However, matrimonial cases are not the only ones in which there might be question of warding off danger of soul. The words employed by the canon are very general: "Ad aliud quodvis animae suae praejudicium avertendum." Hence, whenever, in the prudent estimation of the judge, there is truly a question of preventing a spiritual danger, the *vitandi* and the *tolerati post sententiam* are to be admitted as plaintiffs, but only by proxy.

59 Can. 1646.
60 Can. 2267.
61 Vermeersch-Creusen, *Epitome,* III, n. 79; Blat, *Commentarium,* IV, *De Processibus,* n. 130; Roberti, *De Processibus,* I, n. 205.

With the exception of the cases mentioned above, the *vitandi* and the *tolerati post sententiam* are to be repelled from *acting* in ecclesiastical courts. This prohibition is most useful to break down their contumacy, and consequently to procure what is most advantageous for them, that is, repentance and absolution from the censure. Nor can this prohibition be regarded as unjust, or even as too severe, for the inability of such persons to appear in court as plaintiff is due solely to their own malice, for they can, whenever they so desire, be freed from the censure.[62]

The *vitandi* and the *tolerati post sententiam,* except in cases in which they desire to impugn the justice or the legitimacy of the excommunication, or to avert some other spiritual danger, are to be repelled from acting in ecclesiastical courts. They are to be repelled, because they cannot *validly* be admitted as plaintiffs; they are not entitled to *act* in an ecclesiastical court (*non habent personam standi in judicio*). Consequently, a sentence given in a case, in which such a person was admitted as plaintiff is incurably null ("vitio insanabilis nullitatis laborat").[63]

All other excommunicates, that is, except the *vitandi* and the *tolerati post sententiam,* can generally *stand* in ecclesiastical courts.[64] This provision of law, however, is modified by Canon 1628, § 3, which gives the opposing parties the right to oppose the exception, or the objection of excommunication. The sense of Canon 1654, § 2, is, therefore, that all other excommunicates can stand in ecclesiastical courts, unless the exception of excommunication is brought and proven against them.[65]

All accused excommunicates, when legitimately cited, must answer,[66] either personally or by proxy. Even

---

62 Noval, *De Processibus*, pars 1, *De Judiciis*, n. 262.
63 Can. 1892, n. 2.
64 Can. 1654, § 2.
65 Woywod, *A Practical Commentary on the Code of Canon Law*, II, n. 1628; Noval, *De Processibus*, pars 1, *De Judiciis*, n. 263; Roberti, *De Processibus*, I, n. 205; Vermeersch-Creusen, *Epitome*, III, n. 79.
66 Can. 1646.

though they have chosen a procurator or an advocate, they are bound to be present in person, when the law or the judge demands their personal presence.[67]

The question now arises whether an excommunicate can bring a counter-claim against the plaintiff. A counter-claim (*reconventio*) is an action (*actio*) which the defendant institutes before the same judge and in the same trial for the purpose of disposing of, or lessening, the claim of the plaintiff.[68] Roberti [69] and Noval,[70] looking upon counter-claims as actions, are of the opinion that excommunicates cannot bring counter-claims against a plaintiff. This statement, of course, must be understood in the light of what has already been said concerning excommunicates as plaintiffs, and hence it is to be applied in its full rigor only to the *vitandi* and the *tolerati post sententiam.* There is much to be said for the opinion of Roberti and Noval, especially since Canon 1690 defines a counter-claim as an action. Since, however, counter-claims have somewhat the nature of legitimate defence, it cannot be held for certain that excommunicates are excluded from making use of them, for there is no positive and express legislation to this effect.

III. Discharge of Ecclesiastical Offices

Prohibetur (excommunicatus) ecclesiasticis officiis seu muneribus fungi.

The term *ecclesiastical office* may be understood either in a wide or in a strict sense. In the wide sense of the term, it is any duty that is legitimately exercised for a spiritual end.[71] In the strict acceptation of the term, an ecclesiastical office is a position stably instituted by divine or ecclesiastical authority which is conferred according to Canon Law, and which carries with it some

---

67 Can. 1647.
68 Can. 1690.
69 *De Processibus,* I, n. 205.
70 *De Processibus,* pars I, *De Judiciis,* n. 265.
71 Can. 145, § 1.

participation in the ecclesiastical power of orders or jurisdiction.[72] Canon 145, § 2 states that in law, the term *ecclesiastical office* is to be understood in its strict sense, unless the contrary is apparent from the context.

Canon 2263 is quite in conformity with the law of the Decretals in forbidding excommunicates to discharge ecclesiastical offices and duties. It seems clear from what has already been said that under the law of the Decretals, no excommunicate could licitly discharge any ecclesiastical office or duty.

Canon 2263 states that excommunicates are forbidden to discharge ecclesiastical offices and duties. The canon evidently has reference to ecclesiastical offices, understood both in the strict and in the wide sense of the term. An excommunicate is forbidden to exercise an ecclesiastical office understood in the strict sense of the term, that is, an office implying some participation in the power of orders or of jurisdiction. This prohibition is very closely connected with Canon 2261 which forbids the exercise of the power of orders to excommunicates and with Canon 2264 which forbids them to posit acts of jurisdiction.

Canon 145, § 2 declares that in law the term *ecclesiastical office* is to be understood in its strict sense, unless the contrary is apparent from the context. The canon under discussion, however, clearly indicates that the term is to be understood not only in its strict sense, but also in its wide acceptation. This is evident from the very wording of the canon "officiis seu muneribus." Hence, excommunicates are forbidden to exercise not only an office which implies a participation in the power of orders or of jurisdiction, but likewise any office or duty whatsoever that is assumed for a spiritual purpose.

---

72 Can. 145, § 1.

IV. Use of Privileges

(*Prohibetur excommunicatus*) *concessisque antea ab Ecclesia privilegiis frui.*

A privilege is a special and permanent faculty granted by a superior either against or beyond the common law.[73] Authors mention many divisions of privileges. For our purpose, it will be necessary to note only one division—the division of privileges into personal and real privileges. A personal privilege is one that is granted directly and immediately to a person. A real privilege is one that is directly attached to a thing, place, office or dignity.

An excommunicate is forbidden to enjoy the privileges which were granted him by the Church before he fell under the censure. There is question here of privileges that were obtained before excommunication was incurred, because, generally speaking, privileges are not granted to those who are under ban of excommunication.[74] Privileges are not lost by the censure of excommunication, because, unless otherwise stated, they are considered to be perpetual.[75]

There is question here of all personal privileges, but only personal privileges. Real privileges do not come under this prohibition. Whether an excommunicate can enjoy real privileges depends upon the nature of the privileges and their relations to the other effects of excommunication.[76]

Since habitual faculties which are granted either *in perpetuum*, or for a definite time, or for a certain number of cases, are to be counted as privileges *praeter jus*,[77] it would seem that the disposition of law under discussion is to be applied to such faculties.[78] However,

[73] Cf. Noldin, *Summa Theologiae Moralis*, I, n. 192; Augustine, *Commentary*, I, p. 152.
[74] Cappello, *De Censuris*, n. 152; cf. Can. 2265, § 2.
[75] Can. 70.
[76] Cappello, *De Censuris*, n. 152.
[77] Can. 66, § 1.
[78] Cappello, *De Censuris*, n. 152.

as Cappello very well remarks, when there is question of such faculties, and, in general, of privileges which are not granted merely for the convenience of the individual, an excommunicate will more easily be excused from the observance of this prohibition. Furthermore, the same author is of the opinion that when such faculties and privileges concern the sacraments and sacramentals, excommunicates can employ them licitly, whenever they can licitly administer the sacraments and sacramentals in accordance with Canon 2261.[79] Cipollini concedes probability to this opinion, but seems to favor the negative view-point.[80] It would seem, however, that the opinion of Cappello is to be preferred for there is question here of privileges that are granted, not in favor of the one who possesses them, but in favor of the faithful in general; furthermore, such privileges are *enjoyed,* not by the one who makes use of them, but by the one to whose advantage they are employed.[81]

79 *Ibidem.*

80 "Videretur negandum, quia Ecclesia excommunicatum simpliciter usu privilegiorum privat; concedendo vero ut fideles ex qualibet justa causa ab eo Sacramenta petant vel Sacramentalia, non ideo privilegiorum concedit usum, sed ordinarium tantum permittit ministerium." *De Censuris Latae Sententiae,* n. 65.

81 Cipollini, *loc. cit.*

CHAPTER VI.

The Exercise of Jurisdiction

CANON 2264.

Actus jurisdictionis tam fori externi quam fori interni positus ab excommunicato est illicitus; et, si lata fuerit sententia condemnatoria vel declaratoria, etiam invalidus, salvo praescripto can. 2261, § 3; secus est validus, imo etiam licitus, si a fidelibus petitus sit ad normam mem. can. 2261, § 2.

It has already been seen that in ordinary circumstances excommunicates cannot exercise the power of orders.[1] According to Canon 2264, they cannot in ordinary circumstances place acts of jurisdiction either of the external or of the internal forum.

Ecclesiastical jurisdiction may be defined as "potestas publica regendi homines baptizatos in ordine ad salutem aeternam a Deo vel ab Ecclesia concessa."[2]

The power of jurisdiction is divided by reason of the forum in which it is exercised into jurisdiction of the external forum and jurisdiction of the internal forum. Jurisdiction of the external forum has reference primarily and immediately to the common good and regulates the actions of the faithful to the Church as a visible society. Jurisdiction of the external forum is divided, by reason of the manner in which it is exercised, into judicial and voluntary jurisdiction, according as it is exercised with or without formal judicial procedure.

---

1 *Supra*, p. 88ff.

2 Cf. Noldin, *Summa Theologiae Moralis*, I, n. 128; Vermeersch-Creusen, *Epitome*, I, n. 200; Wernz-Vidal, *Jus Canonicum*, II, n. 48; Maroto, *Institutiones Juris Canonici*, I, n. 573; Kelly, *The Jurisdiction of the Simple Confessor*, p. 12.

Jurisdiction of the internal forum has reference primarily and immediately to the spiritual welfare of the individual and regulates the obligations of conscience *in ordine ad Deum.* Jurisdiction of the internal forum is two-fold, according as it is exercised in the act of sacramental confession (internal sacramental forum), or outside the Sacrament of Penance (internal non-sacramental forum).

Jurisdiction is divided *ratione tituli* into ordinary and delegated jurisdiction. Ordinary jurisdiction is that which is *ipso jure* annexed to an office, so that when one acquires that office, *ipso facto* he acquires the jurisdiction connected with it. Ordinary jurisdiction is either *proper* or *vicarious.* It is proper when the office is a principle one, ex. gr., a bishopric, and is exercised in one's own name; it is *vicarious* when the office is an accessory one, ex. gr., the office of a vicar-general, and is exercised in another's name.[3] Delegated jurisdiction is not *ipso facto* attached to an office, but is obtained by the commission of a competent superior.[4]

PRE-CODE LAW

All excommunicates were deprived of ecclesiastical jurisdiction in such a manner that they could not exercise acts thereof, at least licitly.[5] The reason was because the exercise of jurisdiction is *praecipua cum fidelibus communicatio.* This privation affected even the *tolerati,* who sinned mortally by exercising the power of jurisdiction, unless they were requested by the faithful to do so.[6]

Were excommunicates altogether stripped of the power of jurisdiction, or were they merely forbidden the licit use of it? All authors agreed that the *vitandi* were

3 Can. 197, § 1, § 2. Cf. Kelly, *The Jurisdiction of the Simple Confessor,* p. 14.

4 Can. 197, § 1.

5 C. 4, 35, 36, 37, C. XXIV, q. 1; c. 24, X, *de sententia et re judicata,* II, 27; c. 13, X, *de haereticis,* V, 7; c. 1, *de officio vicarii* I, 13 in VI°; c. 10, *de officio et potestate judicis delegati,* I, 14 in VI°.

6 Schmalzgrueber, pars IV, tit. XXXIX, n. 163.

altogether stripped of ecclesiastical jurisdiction.[7] Consequently, acts of jurisdiction placed by them were invalid. Jurisdiction for the internal forum was restored to them for the extreme necessity of the moment of death.

The *tolerati* were not altogether stripped of the power of jurisdiction, but they were forbidden to exercise acts thereof. Even if they were publicly known to be under ban of excommunication, they could validly exercise jurisdiction, as long as they were not objected to by the faithful. The faithful could prevent their jurisdictional acts from having effect by objecting to them on the score of excommunication and by proving the existence of the censure. The faithful, however, were not obliged to take exception to the *tolerati*.[8] Acts of jurisdiction posited by the *tolerati* at the request of the faithful were not only valid, but licit as well.

The Present Law

Canon 2264 states that an act of jurisdiction of the external as well as the internal forum posited by an excommunicate is illicit; and, if a condemnatory or declaratory sentence has been issued against the excommunicate, it is invalid, saving the exception of Canon 2261, § 3; otherwise, it is valid, and even licit, if requested by the faithful in accordance with Canon 2261, § 2.

All excommunicates are forbidden to place acts of ordinary or delegated jurisdiction either of the external or of the internal forum. Hence, they are forbidden to establish laws, to pass judicial sentences, to grant dispensations, to absolve from sins and censures, etc. In this matter, however, there must be kept in mind the distinction between the *simpliciter tolerati* and the *vitandi* and the *tolerati* against whom a declaratory or condemnatory sentence has been passed.

---

7 Schmalzgrueber, pars IV, tit. XXXIX, n. 164; Suarez, *De Censuris*, disp. XIV, s. 1ss.; Ballerini-Palmieri, *Opus Theologicum Morale*, VII, n. 409; Wernz, VI, n. 194.

8 Schmalzgrueber, pars. IV, tit. XXXIX, n. 165; Suarez, *De Censuris*, disp. XIV, s. 1, n. 15; Wernz, VI, n. 193.

Acts of jurisdiction of either the external or the internal forum placed by the *simpliciter tolerati* are always valid. The Church, in not absolutely depriving the *simpliciter tolerati* of jurisdiction, but merely forbidding them the licit exercise thereof, has in mind the good of the faithful and the tranquillity of their conscience. It is evident that if such excommunicates were incapable of exercising jurisdiction validly, the faithful would be in constant doubt concerning the validity of the jurisdictional acts of their superiors.[9]

Acts of jurisdiction posited by the *simpliciter tolerati* are not only valid, but even licit, if they are requested by the faithful in accordance with Canon 2261, § 2. This canon, as we have already seen, permits the faithful for any just reason to request the *simpliciter tolerati* to administer the sacraments and sacramentals, especially if no other ministers are available. Hence, it must be said that for any just reason the faithful may request the *simpliciter tolerati* to place acts requiring an exercise of the power of jurisdiction, especially if no other competent persons are present. The principal reason which permits the faithful to do so is the absence of others who can exercise jurisdiction licitly. However, it is by no means the only reason; any just cause will suffice; it does not have to be grave.[10]

Almost all authors teach that a reasonably presumed or implicit petition suffices to allow a *simpliciter toleratus* to administer the sacraments and sacramentals licitly (*ratione censurae*).[11] This, of course, includes the imparting of sacramental absolution, which is a jurisdictional act of the internal forum. There seems to be no reason why such an opinion cannot be extended to include acts of jurisdiction of the external forum. Hence, not only when the petition on the part of the faithful is explicit, but likewise when it is implicit or may reasonably be presumed, the *simpliciter tolerati* may place acts

9 Smith, *Elements of Ecclesiastical Law,* III, n. 3235.
10 *Supra,* pp. 91-92.
11 *Supra,* pp. 92-93.

requiring an exercise of the power of jurisdiction of the external as well as of the internal forum.

The delegation of jurisdiction is itself an act of jurisdiction. The excommunicates now under consideration can, of course, validly delegate jurisdiction to others. Such delegation would be illicit, however, unless it was requested either explicitly or implicitly, which would almost always be the case. Whether or not one who is illicitly delegated can licitly exercise the delegation is a debated question. However, there is a probable opinion which maintains that such a one can licitly exercise the delegation.[12]

The *tolerati* against whom either a declaratory or condemnatory sentence has been issued, and, a fortiori, the *vitandi* cannot place acts of jurisdiction either validly or licitly. Prescinding from Canon 2264, it is to be noted that one who possesses ordinary jurisdiction is *ipso facto* deprived of it by the very fact that he becomes a *vitandus;* for a *vitandus* is *ipso facto* deprived of any office to which the power of jurisdiction might be annexed.[13] Hence, the *vitandi* and the *tolerati post sententiam* cannot validly establish laws, pass judicial sentences, inflict censures, absolve from sins or censures, grant dispensations, etc. There is, however, an exception to this law. Even the *vitandi* and the *tolerati post sententiam* can validly and licitly absolve all penitents who are in danger of death from all sins and censures, no matter how they are reserved or how notorious they may be, even if an approved priest is present.[14] For an explanation of this faculty as well as for a discussion of the power of excommunicates over matrimonial impediments, the reader is referred to the commentary on Canon 2261.[15]

---

12 Cappello, *De Censuris*, n. 155.
13 Can. 2266; 208.
14 Can. 2264; 2261, § 1; 882.
15 *Supra*, p. 93ff.; p. 106ff.

Cappello is of the opinion that a very grave cause, outside the danger of death, such as fear of death, avoidance of a grave scandal, etc., would permit the *tolerati post sententiam* to place acts of jurisdiction validly and (*ratione censurae*) licitly.[16]

---

16 "Quoties tamen actus jurisdictionis licite ponitur, urgente mortis periculo vel, ut opinamur, gravissima alia causa, toties validum est." *De Censuris*, n. 157, 10°.

"*Periculo mortis*, ut indubitanter tenemus, aequiparanda est *causa gravissima*, v. g., metus mortis, scandalum grave vitandum, etc." *Ibidem*, 3°.

CHAPTER VII

The Right of Election, Presentation, Nomination: Acquisition and Privation of Dignities, Offices, etc.: Reception of Orders: Pontifical Rescripts

CANON 2265 AND 2266

Canon 2265:

§ 1. Quilibet excommunicatus:

1.° Prohibetur jure eligendi, praesentandi, nominandi;

2.° Nequit consequi dignitates, officia, beneficia, pensiones ecclesiasticas, aliudve munus in Ecclesia;

3.° Promoveri nequit ad ordines.

§ 2. Actus tamen positus contra praescriptum § 1, nn. 1, 2, non est nullus, nisi positus fuerit ab excommunicato vitando vel ab alio excommunicato post sententiam declaratoriam vel condemnatoriam; quod si haec sententia lata fuerit, excommunicatus nequit praeterea gratiam ullam pontificiam valide consequi, nisi in pontificio rescripto mentio de excommunicatione fiat.

Canon 2266:

Post sententiam condemnatoriam vel declaratoriam excommunicatus manet privatus fructibus dignitatis, officii, beneficii, pensionis, muneris, si quod habeat in Ecclesia; et vitandus ipsamet dignitate, officio, beneficio, pensione, munere.

I. THE RIGHT OF ELECTION, PRESENTATION, NOMINATION

CANON 2265, §1, n. 1.

Quilibet excommunicatus prohibetur jure eligendi, praesentandi, nominandi.

An ecclesiastical office in the wide sense of the term is any duty that is legitimately exercised for a spiritual purpose. In the strict sense of the term, an ecclesiastical office is a position stably instituted by divine or ecclesiastical authority which is conferred according to the rules of Canon Law and which carries with it some participation in the ecclesiastical power of orders or of jurisdiction. In Law, the term *ecclesiastical office* is to be understood in its strict signification, unless the contrary is apparent from the context.[1]

An ecclesiastical office cannot be validly obtained without canonical appointment. By canonical appointment is understood the granting of an ecclesiastical office by competent ecclesiastical authority according to the regulations of Canon Law.[2]

Appointment to an ecclesiastical office is made: (1) by free appointment (*libera collatio*); (2) by institution, when presentation by a patron or nomination has preceded (*collatio necessaria*); (3) by confirmation or admission, if election or postulation has preceded; (4) by simple election and acceptation by the one elected, if the election does not require confirmation.[3] Hence it is evident that some can enjoy the right of electing, presenting, or nominating a person for an ecclesiastical office.

Election in the strict canonical sense of the term, as distinct from other modes of appointment to ecclesiastical office, is defined as: "personae idoneae ad ecclesiasticum officium vacans per eos quibus jus suffragii competit, canonice facta vocatio."[4]

---

1 Can. 145, §§ 1, 2.
2 Can. 147, §§ 1, 2.
3 Can. 148, § 1.
4 Wernz, II, n. 352.

Presentation may be defined as: "jus designandi et offerendi clericum idoneum ab Episcopo vel competente Praelato in officio ecclesiastico vacante necessario instituendum."[5] The right of presentation usually has place in the *juspatronatus*. Thus Canon 1455 numbers among the privileges of patrons that of presenting a cleric for a vacant church or benefice. It has been said that the right of presentation *usually* has place in the *juspatronatus*. It is to be noted that sometimes the Holy See grants either by concordat or in some other manner an indult of presenting to a vacant church or parish. This indult, however, does not give rise to the *juspatronatus*, and the privilege of presentation must be interpreted strictly according to the tenor of the indult.[6] It is to be noted that sometimes the person to be presented is designated by election. This is the case when the right of patronage is exercised by a college or body of patrons.[7] It is likewise the case when several patrons have an individual right of presentation and cannot agree as to alternate presentation.[8]

The term *nomination* is sometimes used in a very general sense to signify any kind of provision for an ecclesiastical office. Hence it is often confused with election and presentation.[9] In its strict sense, it signifies either the designation of a person for an ecclesiastical office which precedes formal presentation to the Superior, or the exercise of the right of presentation which is founded, not on the *juspatronatus*, but on an Apostolic indult.[10] There are two kinds of nomination which can concur with election—consultory or less solemn nomination, and solemn nomination. The former is a sort of

---

5 *Ibidem.*

6 Can. 1471.

7 Can. 1460, § 1.

8 Can. 1460, § 2.

9 Maroto, *Institutiones Juris Canonici*, I, n. 610; Wernz, II, n. 352; Cappello, *De Censuris*, n. 153.

10 "Strictiore vero sensu nominatio significat aut *designationem personae* promovendae, quae *formali praesentationi* personae Superiori factae praecedit aut exercitationem juris praesentandi, quatenus illud nititur *privilegio apostolico*, non jure patronatus." (Wernz, II, n. 352.

inquiry, which precedes election properly so-called, by which several capable candidates are proposed, upon whom the electors vote. Solemn nomination is that by which two or more candidates are proposed by a body of electors and presented to the Superior who chooses one of them. In solemn nomination, it is not necessary that the persons who are to be presented be designated by election properly so-called. Any manner of designation which has the unanimous consent of all the electors present may be employed.[11]

The Former Discipline

The *vitandi* could not validly exercise the right of voting. Votes cast by the *tolerati,* however, were valid, unless exception was taken to their participation in the election.[12] No excommunicate could licitly present a candidate for an ecclesiastical office; if the excommunicate was a *vitandus,* the presentation was invalid and could not be admitted by the superior; if the excommunicate was a *toleratus,* the superior could admit the presentation, but he was not obliged to do so.[13] The same was true of nomination.[14]

The Present Law

All excommunicated persons are forbidden to exercise the right of election, presentation and nomination. The prohibition affects the *tolerati* as well as the *vitandi.* Acts, however, which are posited in violation of this prohibition, are not invalid, unless they are posited by the *vitandi* or the *tolerati* against whom a declaratory or condemnatory sentence has been pronounced.[15]

When the person to be appointed to an ecclesiastical office is designated by election properly so-called, a vote cast by a *vitandus* or a *toleratus post sententiam* is in-

11 Maroto, *Institutiones Juris Canonici,* I, n. 610; Wernz, II, n. 352.

12 Wernz, II, n. 357, not. 29; cf. c. 23, X, *de appellationibus, etc.,* II, 28; c. unic., *ne sede vacante,* III, 8 in VI°.

13 Wernz, II, n. 440; cf. Suarez, *De Censuris,* disp. XIV, s. 2, n. 30ss.

14 Suarez, *De Censuris,* disp, XIV, s. 2, n. 32.

15 Can. 2265, § 2.

valid. The election itself, however, is valid, except in two cases: (1) when it is certain that the vote of the excommunicate was decisive, that is, when it is certain that without the vote of the excommunicate, the person elected would not have received a sufficient number of votes to gain the election; (2) when the excommunicate was knowingly (*scienter*) admitted to the election.[16]

It would seem by virtue of Canon 20 that the same principle would govern the cases in which the person to be presented or nominated for an ecclesiastical office is determined by vote.

II. Acquisition and Privation of Dignities, etc.

Canon 2265, § 1, n. 2.

Quilibet excommunicatus nequit consequi dignitates, officia, beneficia, pensiones ecclesiasticas aliudve munus in Ecclesia.

Canon 2266.

Post sententiam condemnatoriam vel declaratoriam excommunicatus manet privatus fructibus dignitatis, officii, beneficii, pensionis, numeris, si quod habeat in Ecclesia; et vitandus ipsamet dignitate, officio, beneficio, pensione, munere.

A *dignity* is generally a benefice to which, besides the prerogatives of honor and precedence, there was formerly attached some jurisdiction in the external forum. At the present time, a dignity very seldom carries with it any jurisdiction.[17]

The term *ecclesiastical office* has already been considered.[18]

A *benefice* is a juridical being constituted or erected *in perpetuum* by competent ecclesiastical authority, con-

16 Can. 167, § 2.

17 Vermeersch-Creusen, *Epitome*, I, n. 449; Cappello, *De Censuris*, n. 154; Chelodi, *Jus de Personis*, n. 204; Augustine, *Commentary*, II, p. 426.

18 *Supra*, pp. 140-141.

sisting of a sacred office and the right of receiving the revenue from the endowment of the office.[19]

An *ecclesiastical pension* may be described as the "jus percipiendi partem fructuum alicujus beneficii vel mensae, titulo non perpetuo."[20]

The term *aliudve munus* may be understood of any office or duty that is constituted or exercised for a spiritual purpose.[21]

The Pre-code Discipline

Under the law of the Decretals,[22] excommunicates were incapable of acquiring any benefice, or ecclesiastical office whatsoever. The reason for this was because excommunicates were forbidden to exercise ecclesiastical offices and to communicate with the faithful. Hence with reason were they excluded from the acquisition of any position which required the performance of ecclesiastical functions and communication with the people.[23] It was the common teaching of canonists that this exclusion extended even to the *tolerati.* D'Annibale, however, against the opinion which he himself admitted to be the commonly accepted one, raised some doubt about the incapacity of the *tolerati* to acquire benefices, offices, etc. He thought it more reasonable to hold that the *tolerati* were capable of acquiring benefices, etc.[24] Wernz saw in this proposal of D'Annibale merely an effort to bring about a change in the *jus vigens.* Wernz admitted that many and grave inconveniences could arise from the fact that the appointment of an occult excommunicate to a benefice, office, etc. was invalid. He suggested that this could be remedied by making such an appointment invalid only in the case of an excommunicate *post sen-*

19 Can. 1409.

20 Vermeersch-Creusen, *Epitome,* I, n. 207; cf. Reiffenstuel, lib. III, tit. 5, n. 84ss.

21 Cappello, *De Censuris,* n. 154.

22 Cf. Schmalzgrueber, pars IV, tit. XXXIX, n. 147ss.; Suarez, *De Censuris,* disp. XIII; Wernz, VI, n. 193.

23 Schmalzgrueber, *loc. cit.*

24 *Summula Theologiae Moralis,* I, n. 365.

tentiam.[25] It will be seen that the Code has followed this suggestion.

Pensions granted for the exercise of some spiritual function could not be conferred validly upon excommunicates, for all excommunicates were forbidden to perform any ecclesiastical function. There was disagreement among authors concerning pensions granted for some reason other than the exercise of spiritual functions, ex. gr., to a cleric who resigned a benefice, to one not having sufficient sustentation otherwise. Some maintained that such pensions could not validly be conferred upon excommunicates, while others were of the affirmative opinion.[26]

Excommunicates were not *ipso facto* deprived of the benefices, offices, etc., which they had obtained before incurring the censure. It was disputed among authors whether they were *ipso facto* and *ante sententiam* deprived of the fruits of benefices, offices, etc.[27]

The Present Law

The Code sets forth the legislation concerning excommunicates and the acquisition and privation of ecclesiastical dignities, offices, benefices, pensions, etc., in such clear and unmistakable terms that very little comment will have to be made upon it.

No excommunicate can acquire dignities, offices, benefices, ecclesiastical pensions, or any other position in the Church. The acquisition of such, however, is not invalid, except in the case of a *vitandus* or a *toleratus* against whom a declaratory or condemnatory sentence has been passed (Can. 2265, § 2).

After a condemnatory or declaratory sentence, an excommunicate is deprived (*manet privatus*) of the fruits of a dignity, office, benefice, pension, or any other position he may have in the Church (Can. 2266). This priva-

25 VI, n. 193, not. 306.

26 Cf. Schmalzgrueber, pars IV, tit. XXXIX, n. 153.

27 Cf. c. 53, X, *de appellationibus,* II, 28; Schmalzgrueber, pars IV, tit. XXXIX, n. 158; Suarez, *De Censuris,* disp. XIII, s. 2, n. 1ss.; Wernz, VI, n. 193; Holweck, pp. 121-122, § 47, not. 6.

tion is incurred by the very fact that a condemnatory or declaratory sentence has been issued against the person. No specific sentence to this effect is required. Most canonists are of the opinion that in the case of a declaratory sentence, this privation retroacts to the time when the censure was incurred.[28] They base their opinion on Canon 2232, § 2, which states: "Sententia declaratoria poenam ad momentum commissi delicti retrotrahit." Vermeersch-Creusen, however, maintain that the privation does not retroact to the time of the commission of the delict. They argue from the very wording of the canon, "post sententiam . . . manet privatus."[29] Cocchi seems to be of the same opinion.[30] This latter opinion seems to be probable not only extrinsically by reason of the authors who embrace it, but also intrinsically by reason of the wording of the canon "post sententiam . . . manet privatus."

III. The Reception of Orders

Quilibet excommunicatus promoveri nequit ad ordines.

Orders may be defined as "Sacramentum Novae Legis quo spiritualis traditur potestas et confertur gratia ad conficiendam Eucharistiam, aliaque ecclesiastica munia rite obeunda."[31] There are seven orders, three of which are called major or sacred orders and the remaining four are called minor orders. The three major or sacred orders are subdeaconship, deaconship and priesthood: the priesthood comprises the dignity of simple priest and that of bishop. The four minor orders are those of porter, lector, exorcist and acolyte.

Episcopal consecration, priesthood and deaconship are sacraments, that is, *rationem habent sacramenti.*[32]

---

[28] Cappello, *De Censuris*, n. 157; Chelodi, *Jus Poenale*, n. 38; Augustine, *Commentary*, VIII, p. 192; Ayrinhac, *Penal Legislation*, p. 74.

[29] *Epitome*, III, n. 468.

[30] *Commentarium*, VIII, n. 88.

[31] Tanquerey, *Synopsis Theologiae Dogmaticae*, III, n. 797.

[32] Cf. C. of Trent, sess. XXIII, can. 3-4; Gasparri, *De Sacra Ordinatione*, n. 39; Pesch, *Praelectiones Dogmaticae*, VII, n. 597ss., n. 606ss., 613ss.; Tanquerey, *Synopsis Theologiae Dogmaticae*, III, n. 808-814.

Whether subdeaconship and the minor orders are sacraments was at one time a much debated question. It would seem that the negative opinion is more commonly accepted by theologians at the present time.[33] The defenders of this opinion argue that these orders are of ecclesiastical origin and that the Church cannot attach grace to an external sign; furthermore, in the conferment of subdeaconship and the minor orders, there is no imposition of hands which is an essential rite of the Sacrament of Orders.[34]

There is a ceremony called Tonsure which serves as a preparation for the reception of orders. It is a sacred rite, instituted by the Church, by which a man is enrolled among the clergy and dedicated to God in a special manner that he might dispose himself for the reception of orders.[35] Tonsure is not a sacrament; it is not even an order. However, according to Canon 950, in law the terms *ordinare, ordo, ordinatio, sacra ordinatio* comprehend, besides episcopal consecration and the three major and the four minor orders, the first tonsure, unless the contrary is evident from the nature of the matter or from the context.

The very nature of the censure of excommunication has always forbidden those under its ban to receive orders. Excommunication separates one from communication with others, especially in divine matters. Hence since the various clerical orders are directed to communication in divine matters with others, it is clear that no excommunicate can licitly receive orders.[36] In the very rite of ordination, excommunicates are forbidden under pain of excommunication to approach to receive orders.[37]

---

33 Perrone, *Praelectiones Theologicae,* VII, *Tractatus de Ordine,* cap. II, n. 81; Franzelin, *Tractatus de Divina Traditione et Scriptura,* sect. II, cap. II, th. XVII; Gasparri, *De Sacra Ordinatione,* n. 41; Pesch, *Praelectiones Dogmaticae,* VII, n. 585ss., 592ss.

34 Tanquerey, *Synopsis Theologiae Dogmaticae,* III, n. 815.

35 Tanquerey, *Synopsis Theologiae Dogmaticae,* III, n. 840.

36 Gasparri, *De Sacra Ordinatione,* n. 141.

37 Pontificale Romanum, tit., *De Ordinibus Conferendis.*

Innocent III wrote of those who had incurred excommunication for laying violent hands upon clerics who, "ecclesiasticam sententiam negligentes, in excommunicatione positi ecclesiasticos ordines accipere non formidant." He decreed that a secular cleric who knowingly did so was to be deposed; a religious was to be suspended from the exercise of the order. If a secular cleric, thus excommunicated, ignorant either of the law or of the fact, received orders, only the Pope could dispense him; if a religious did so under the same circumstances the abbot could dispense him, if ignorance could be presumed and the fact was not grave.[38]

Canon 2265, § 1, n. 3 states that no excommunicate can be promoted to orders. The term *ordines* in this canon comprises episcopal consecration, the three major and the four minor orders and even tonsure.[39] The canon under discussion is very closely connected with Canon 2260, which denies to excommunicates the passive use of the sacraments and sacramentals. However, it is more extensive that Canon 2260. Canon 2260 forbids the reception of the sacramentals only to excommunicated persons against whom a declaratory or condemnatory sentence has been pronounced. Canon 2265, § 1, n. 3 forbids all excommunicates to receive even tonsure, the minor orders and subdeaconship, which are, according to the more common opinion, sacramentals and not sacraments.

Orders received by excommunicates are valid. This is true not only of those orders whose reception constitutes a sacrament, that is, episcopal consecration, priesthood and deaconship, but also of subdeaconship, minor orders and tonsure. The validity of the former depends on what is required by divine law; the validity of the latter depends on the requisites of ecclesiastical law; and the Church has not placed freedom from excommunication as an essential condition for their valid rception.[40]

---

38 C. 32, X, *de sententia excommunicationis*, V. 39.

39 Can. 950; Cocchi, *Commentarium*, VIII, n. 87; Blat, *Commentarium*, V, *De Delictis et Poenis*, n. 92; Augustine, *Commentary*, VIII, p. 191.

40 Cf. Blat, *Commentarium*, V, *De Delictis et Poenis*, n. 92.

IV. Pontifical Rescripts

Quod si haec sententia lata fuerit, excommunicatus nequit praeterea gratiam ullam pontificiam valide consequi, nisi in pontificio rescripto mentio de excommunicatione fiat.

A rescript is a response given in writing by the Holy See or an Ordinary to a question asked or a favor requested.[41] It will be necessary for our purpose to take into consideration the division of rescripts *ratione objecti* into rescripts of justice and rescripts of grace. A rescript of justice is a response which contains a provision relating to a judicial controversy or to the administration of justice. A rescript of grace is one that contains a favor; it may grant a simple grace, privilege or a dispensation.[42]

Under the law of the Decretals, excommunicates were *ipso jure* incapable of validly acquiring any pontifical rescript either of justice or of grace.[43] This disability affected all excommunicates without exception, the *tolerati* as well as the *vitandi,* occult excommunicates as well as those whose excommunication was a matter of public knowledge.[44] There were exceptions to this rule with regard to rescripts relating to the cause of excommunication and appeal from it.[45] Therefore, lest on account of excommunication, a rescript be invalid, it was the practice of the Roman Curia to absolve the petitioners *ad cautelam* from censures, but only to the effect that the rescript might be valid—"ad effectum dumtaxat gratiae consequendae."[46]

Absolution *ad cautelam* is an absolution which exercises its influence only in cases in which there is a censure

---

41 Cf. Can. 36, § 1; Wernz, I, n. 150; Vermeersch-Creusen, *Epitome,* I, n. 123; Augustine, *Commentary,* I, p. 124.

42 Can. 62.

43 C. 26, X, *de rescriptis,* I, 3; c. 1, *de rescriptis,* I, 3 in VI°

44 Wernz, I, n. 151; Chelodi, *Jus de Personis,* n. 76.

45 "Ipso jure rescriptum, vel processus per ipsum habitus, non valeat, si ab excommunicato super alio quam excommunicationis vel appeallationis articulo fuerit impetratum." C. 1, *de rescriptis,* I, 3 in VI°.

46 Wernz, I, n. 151.

which would otherwise invalidate the rescript: it is an absolution only for its proper effect, that is, it does not remove the censure completely and absolutely, but only, as it were, *secundum quid.* It simply causes the censure to be no longer a hindrance to the valid attainment of a rescript and leaves the other effects of the censure as they were.[47]

At one time, this absolution *ad cautelam* did not benefit those who had incurred excommunication either *a jure* or *ab homine* for certain delicts mentioned in the Rules of the Apostolic Chancery, and "per quatuor menses scienter excommunicationis sententiam sustinuerint (insorduerint)." In like manner it did not benefit persons who had contumaciously lived under any censure for the period of a year (*insorduerint*).[48] However, the number of persons who were excluded from this benefit of absolution *ad cautelam* was greatly reduced by the Constitution *"Apostolicae Sedis,"* which abrogated many of the *latae sententiae* censures formerly in vogue. Furthermore, it would seem that persons who had lived contumaciously under censure for a year were deprived of the benefit of absolution *ad cautelam* only if they had been publicly excommunicated and nominally denounced.[49]

A rather interesting response was given by the Sacred Penitentiary on September 8, 1898. A certain priest, while under ban of a reserved excommunication that was occult, had asked and obtained from the Roman Congregations rescripts granting minor graces, ex. gr., to read forbidden books, to bless rosaries, etc. with the application of indulgences, etc. Hearing that excommunicates were incapable of obtaining Papal graces, he became somewhat disturbed, and the following questions were proposed: (1) whether such rescripts obtained while under ban of excommunication were valid; (2) in case

---

47 DeSmet, *De Sponsalibus et Matrimonio*, n. 878, not. 2.

48 Reg. 66.

49 Wernz, I, n. 151, not. 31; Konings-Putzer, *Commentarium in Facultates Apostolicas*, n. 46.

they were invalid, how should the priest conduct himself in order not to manifest the reason why the rescripts were invalid. The Sacred Penitentiary replied: "Orator super praemissis acquiescat. Pro foro conscientiae tantum."[50]

It was the *Normae Peculiares* of the Roman Curia, published in conjunction with the Constitution "*Sapienti consilio*," that effected an important change in this matter. In Chapter III, n. 6 of the *Normae Peculiares,* it was decreed that all favors and dispensations granted by the Holy See after November 3, 1908, on which day the Constitution "*Sapienti consilio*" began to have the force of law, were valid and legitimate, even if granted to persons under ban of censure, with the exception of those who were nominally excommunicated, or whom the Holy See had nominally suspended *a divinis.*[51]

Hence no longer were all excommunicates incapable of validly acquiring Papal rescripts. After November 3, 1908, this disability affected only those who were nominally excommunicated. A person was considered to be nominally excommunicated when the Superior, either expressly mentioning him by name, or otherwise designating him that he could not be confounded with others, declared that he was under ban of excommunication. It did not matter whether the declaration came from the Holy See or another competent ecclesiastical authority, nor whether the excommuncation was incurred only at the time of the declaration, or previously.[52]

This legislation with but few changes has been incorporated into the Code.

Canon 36, § 2 states that all graces and dispensations granted by the Holy See, even to those under censure,

---

50 *Analecta Ecclesiastica,* 1903, t. XI, p. 421.

51 *AAS,* I, (1909); "* * * a die III mensis Novembris MDCCCCVIII, quo die incipient vim legis habere praescripta in constitutione *Sapienti consilio,* gratiae ac dispensationes omne genus a Sancta Sede concessae, etiam censura irretitis, ratae ac legitimae, nisi de iis agatur qui nominatim excommunicati sint, aut a Sancta Sede nominatim pariter poena suspensionis a divinis multati."

52 Martin, *The Roman Curia,* pp. 268-269.

are valid, with due regard, however, to Canons 2265, § 2, 2275, n. 3, and 2283. Our present interest concerns Canon 2265, § 2, which says that if a declaratory or condemnatory sentence has been pronounced against an excommunicate, he cannot validly obtain any pontifical *favor,* unless mention is made of the excommunication in the pontifical rescript.

Some doubt may arise as to whether Canon 2265, § 2 is meant to include privileges and dispensations.[53] Canon 36, § 2 and Canon 62 give rise to this doubt. The former expressly distinguishes between graces and dispensations, while the latter expressly distinguished between a simple grace, dispensation and privilege. It seems certain, however, that Canon 2265, § 2 has reference not only to simple graces or favors, but likewise to privileges and dispensations as well. The words *gratia ulla* indicate this, for privileges and dispensations are commonly included under the name of graces and favors.[54]

With regard to the excommunicates who are excluded from validly obtaining papal favors, the Code is substantially in conformity with the *Normae Peculiares,* published in conjunction with the Constitution "*Sapienti consilio.*" As has been seen, the latter excluded all persons who were excommunicated by name. The Code excludes the *vitandi* and the *tolerati* against whom a declaratory or condemnatory sentence has been pronounced.

Rescripts of grace granted by the Holy See to the *vitandi* or the *tolerati* against whom a declaratory or condemnatory sentence has been issued are invalid "unless, in the Papal rescript, mention be made of the censure, implying that the concession is made in spite of it or unless an absolution from censures, called *ad effectum,* be inserted in the rescript for the purpose of securing its validity."[55]

---

53 Cappello, *De Censuris,* n. 157; Cocchi, *Commentarium,* VIII, n. 88.
54 Cappello and Cocchi, *loc cit.*
55 Ayrinhac, *Penal Legislation,* p. 126.

There is question in the legislation under discussion only of pontifical graces, that is, graces and favors granted either directly by the Pope, or by a Congregation of the Roman Curia. Hence favors that might be conceded to excommunicates by an authority inferior to the Holy See would not be null by virtue of Canon 2265, § 2.[56]

It may be noted here that notorious excommunicates cannot validly be received into associations of the faithful, such as, secular tertiary orders, confraternities and pious unions.[57] Should a member of such associations become a notorious excommunicate, after due warning he should be expelled in the manner provided in the statutes; such a one, however, retains the right of having recourse to the Ordinary.[58]

---

56 Cappello, *De Censuris*, n. 157; Chelodi, *Jus Poenale*, n. 38; Cocchi, *Commentarium*, VIII, n. 88.

57 Can. 693, § 1.

58 Can. 696, § 2.

CHAPTER VIII.

Indirect Effects of Excommunication

Besides the immediate or direct effects of excommunication which have just been discussed at length, it remains to say a few words concerning two other effects which excommunication can produce, namely, irregularity and the suspicion of heresy. These are called mediate or indirect, sometimes remote, effects of excommunication, that is, they do not follow immediately or directly from the censure, but they are brought about only when the person under ban of excommunication occasions them.

I. Irregularity

An irregularity is a canonical impediment, of itself perpetual, which *per se* and primarily forbids the reception of orders, and secondarily their exercise.[1] Irregularities are divided into irregularities *ex defectu* and irregularities *ex delicto*.[2] The irregularity *ex defectu* results from certain defects which would be unbecoming in one performing the functions of the sacred ministry. The irregularity *ex delicto* arises from certain delicts which render the guilty one unworthy to receive or to exercise orders.[3] An irregularity *ex delicto* is not contracted unless the delict was a grave sin, committed after baptism (except in the case of one, who, outside extreme necessity, allowed himself to be baptized by a non-Catholic), and likewise external, whether public or occult.[4]

Canon 985, n. 7 states that they are irregular *ex delicto* who, either without the order, or prohibited from its

1 Vermeersch-Creusen, *Epitome*, II, n. 252.
2 Cf. Can. 983.
3 Hickey, *Irregularities and Simple Impediments*, p. 13.
4 Can. 986.

exercise by an canonical punishment, place an act of orders that is reserved to a cleric constituted in sacred orders. In the pre-Code discipline there was an irregularity attached to the violation of a censure. No mention is made of this irregularity in the Decree of Gratian and in parts of the Decretals it is not newly introduced but presupposed.[5] Hence it would seem that this irregularity arose rather from custom than from written law.[6]

In the first place, it may be noted that the irregularity spoken of in Canon 985, n. 7 affects not only members of the clerical state, but laymen as well. Consequently, laymen and clerics, not in sacred orders, become irregular if they exercise an order reserved to one in sacred orders. However, our present interest in Canon 985, n. 7 concerns the irregularity which results from a violation of some of the effects of excommunication, and this irregularity is contracted only by clerics in sacred orders. Should an excommunicate in sacred orders place an act of sacred orders that is forbidden him by the censure, he becomes irregular *ex delicto.* Of course, an excommunicate in sacred orders who exercises the functions of sacred orders under the circumstances laid down in Canon 2261, § 2 and § 3 does not contract an irregularity.

II. Suspicion of Heresy

Formerly one who contumaciously remained under excommunication for a year (*insordescebat*) was subject to certain extraordinary effects, such as the privation of a benefice *per sententiam,*[7] suspicion of heresy,[8] and invocation of the secular arms.[9]

---

5 C. 10, X, *de cler. excom.*, V, 27; c. 1, *de sent. et re jud.* II, 14 in VI°; c. 1, 18, 20, *de sent. excom.*, V, 11 in VI°.

6 Wernz, II, n. 136, not. 334.

7 Cf. c. 8, X, *de aet. et qual. ord.* I, 14; Suarez, *De Censuris*, disp. XVII, s. 1, n. 7; Schmalzgrueber, pars IV, tit. XXXIX, n. 197; Ballerini-Palmieri, *Opus Theologicum Morale*, VII, n. 374ss.; Wernz, VI, n. 197; Crnica, *Modificationes in Tractatu de Censuris*, p. 103.

8 C. 13, X, *de haeret.* V, 7; c. 13, X, *de poenis*, V, 37; c. 7, *de haeret.* V, 2 in VI°; Conc. Trid., sess. XXV, *de ref.*, c. 3.

9 C. 2, X, *de cler. exc.* V, 27; Wernz, VI, n. 197; Crnica, *op. cit.*, p. 103.

At the present time, according to Canon 2340, § 1, one who continues obstinately in the censure of excommunication for a year is suspected of heresy. This suspicion of heresy arises from this that one who contumaciously remains under the censure of excommunication for a year seems to contemn the authority of the Church and to think little of the spiritual goods of which he is deprived by the censure.[10] In order that this suspicion of heresy arise, it would seem that the excommunication must be notorious at least by fact.[11] Cipollini, however, is of the opinion that this suspicion of heresy affects only the *vitandi* and the *tolerati* against whom a condemnatory or declaratory sentence has been pronounced. "Nam hujusmodi praesumptio fori externi est et juridica praesumptio, quae non sustinetur nisi in foro externo, nisi scilicet juridice constet eum esse excommunicatum. At quomodo de hoc constabit sine sententia?"[12]

Those who are suspected of heresy are to be warned to remove the cause of the suspicion; if they neglect to do so, they are to be prohibited from legitimate acts, and besides this, a cleric, who does not heed a second admonition, is to be suspended *a divinis;* if those who are suspected of heresy do not amend within six months after they have contracted the penalty, they are to be considered as heretics, subject to the punishments of heretics.[13]

---

10 Cf. Suarez, *De Censuris,* disp. XVII, s. 1, n. 6; Sole, *De Delictis et Poenis,* n. 369; Cipollini, *De Censuris Latae Sententiae,* n. 71; Vermeersch-Creusen, *Epitome,* III, n. 539.

11 Cocchi, *Commentarium,* VIII, n. 180; Vermeersch-Creusen, *Epitome,* III, n. 539.

12 *De Censuris Latae Sententiae,* n. 71.

13 Can. 2315.

BIBLIOGRAPHY

Sources

Acta Apostolicae Sedis, Romae, 1909

Acta Sanctae Sedis, 41 vols., Romae, 1865-1908.

Canones et Decreta Concilii Tridentini, Taurini, 1913.

Codex Juris Canonici Pii X Pontificis Maximi jussu digestus Benedicti Papae XV auctoritate promulgatus, Romae, 1918.

Codicis Juris Canonici Fontes, 4 vols., Romae, 1923-1926.

Collectanea S. Congregationis de Propaganda Fide, 2 vols., Romae, 1907.

Corpus Juris Canonici, editio Lipsiensis secunda, 2 vols., Lipsiae, 1922.

Denzinger & Bannwart, *Enchiridion Symbolorum,* Friburgi Brisgoviae, 1922.

Mansi, Joannes, *Sacrorum Conciliorum Nova et Amplissima Collectio,* 51 vols., Parisiis, 1902-1924.

Missale Romanum, Ratisbonae, 1925.

Pontificale Romanum, Ratisbonae, 1908.

Rituale Romanum, Ratisbonae, 1894; 1926.

Reference Works

A Coronata, Matthaeus, *De Locis et Temporibus Sacris,* Augustae Taurinorum, 1922.

Aertnys, Joseph, *Theologia Moralis,* 3 ed., 2 vols., Tornaci, 1893.

Aertnys-Damen, Theologia Moralis, 10 ed., 2 vols., Buscoduci, 1919-1920.

A Lapide, Cornelius, *The Great Commentary of,* translated by T. W. Mossman, 7 vols., London, 1887-1890.

ALTERIUS MARIUS, *Disputationes de Censuris Ecclesiasticis*, Romae, 1616.

Analecta Ecclesiastica, Romae, an. 1903.

Ante-Nicene Christian Library, edited by Roberts and Donaldson, vol. XVII, Edinburgh, 1870.

AUGUSTINE, CHARLES, *A Commentary on the New Code of Canon Law*, 8 vols., St. Louis, 1918-1922.

AYRINHAC, H. A., *Marriage Legislation in the New Code of Canon Law*, New York, 1918.

——————, *Penal Legislation in the New Code of Canon Law*, New York, 1920.

BALLERINI-PALMIERI, *Opus Thelogicum Morale*, 7 vols., Prati, 1893.

BELLERMINUS, ROBERTUS, *Opera Omnia*, 5 vols., Parisiis, 1870.

BENEDICTUS XIV, *De Synodo Diocesana*, 2 vols., Romae, 1806.

BERARDI, C., *Commentaria in Jus Ecclesiasticum Universum*, Mediolani, 1847.

BILLOT, LUDOVICUS, *Tractatus de Ecclesia Christi*, vol. I, 3 ed., Prati, 1909.

BINGHAM, JOSEPH, *The Works of*, 10 vols., Oxford, 1855.

BLAT, ALBERTUS, *Commentarium Textus Codicis Juris Canonici*, 5 vols., Romae, 1921-1927.

BONACINA, MARTINUS, *Operum Omnium de Morali Theologia Compendium Absolutissimum*, Lugduni, 1634.

BUCCERONI, J., *Commentarius de Censuris*, Romae, 1885.

CAESAR, *De Bello Gallico*.

CAPPELLO, FELIX, *Tractatus Canonico-Moralis de Censuris juxta Codicem Juris Canonici*, 2 ed., Taurinorum Augustae, 1925.

——————, *Tractatus Canonico-Moralis de Sacramentis;* vol. I, *De Sacramentis in Genere, de Baptismo, Confirmatione, Eucharistia*, 2 ed., Taurinorum Augustae, 1928; vol. II, pars I, *De Poenitentia*, Taurinorum Augustae, 1926; vol. III, *De Matrimonio*, 2 ed., Romae, 1927.

Catholic Encyclopedia, 15 vols., New York, 1913.

CERATO, PROSDOCIMUS, *Censurae Vigentes Ipso Facto a Codice Juris Canonici Excerptae*, Patavii, 1918.

————, *Matrimonium a Codice Juris Canonici Integre Desumptum*, 4 ed., Patavii, 1927.

CHELODI, JOANNES, *Jus de Personis*, 2 ed., Tridenti, 1927.

————, *Jus Matrimoniale*, 3 ed., Tridenti, 1921.

————, *Jus Poenale*, Tridenti, 1920.

CIPOLLINI, ALBERTUS, *De Censuris Latae Sententiae juxta Codicem Juris Canonici*, Taurini, 1925.

COCCHI, GUIDUS, *Commentarium in Codicem Juris Canonici*, 7 vols., Taurinorum Augustae, 1925.

CRAISSON, D., *Manuale Totius Juris Canonici*, Pictavii, 1875.

CRNICA, ANTONIUS, *Modificationes in Tractatu de Censuris per Codicem Juris Canonici introductae*, S. Mauritii Agaunensis, 1919.

CRONIN, CHARLES, *The New Matrimonial Legislation* (a commentary on the *Ne Temere*), 2 ed., New York, 1910.

D'ANNIBALE, JOSEPH, *Summula Theologiae Moralis*, Vol. I, 3 ed., Romae, 1888.

DE LUGO, JOANNES, *Disputationes Scholasticae et Moralis*, 8 vols., Parisiis, 1868-1869.

DE SMEDT, CAROLUS, *Dissertationes Selectae in Primam Aetatem Historiae Ecclesiasticae*, Gandavi, 1876.

DE SMET, ALOYSIUS, *Tractatus Theologico-Canonicus de Sponsalibus et Matrimonio*, 4 ed., Brugis, 1927.

DEVOTI, JOANNES, *Libri IV Institutionum Canonicarum*, Leodii, 1860.

Dictionnaire Encyclopédique de la Théologie Catholique, 26 vols., Paris, 1858-1868.

DIXON, JOSEPH, *A General Introduction to the Sacred Scriptures*, 2 vols., Baltimore, 1853.

DUCHESNE, MSGR. L., *Christian Worship; Its Origin and Evolution*, translated from third French edition by M. L. McClure, London, 1903.

Encyclopedia Brittanica, 12 ed., 32 vols., Cambridge, 1922.

ESTIUS GUILIELMUS, *In Omnes Pauli Epistolas, itemque in Catholicas Commentarii*, 7 vols., Moguntiae, 1841-1845.

FARRUGIA, NICOLAUS, *De Matrimonio et Causis Matrimonialibus*, Taurini-Romae, 1924.

FERRERES, JOANNES, *Compendium, Theologiae Moralis ad Norman Codicis Juris Canonici*, 6 ed., 3 vols., Barcinone, 1925.

FRANZELIN, JOANNES, *Tractatus de Divina Traditione et Scriptura*, Romae, 1870.

GASPARRI, PETRUS, *Tractatus Canonicus de Matrimonio*, 3 ed., 2 vols., Parisiis, 1904.

——————, *Tractatus Canonicus de Sanctissima Eucharistia*, 2 vols., Parisiis, 1897.

——————, *Tractatus Canonicus de Sacra Ordinatione*, 2 vols., Parisiis, 1893-1894.

GENICOT-SALSMANS, *Institutiones Theologiae Moralis*, 7 ed., 2 vols., Bruxellis, 1911; 10 ed., 2 vols., Bruxellis, 1922.

GURY-BALLERINI, *Compendium Theologiae Moralis*, 10 ed., 2 vols., Romae, 1889.

HAGEDORN, FRANCIS, *General Legislation on Indulgences*, Washington, 1924.

HEFELE, CHARLES, *A History of the Christian Councils* (to A. D. 325), translated and edited by W. R. Clark, Edinburgh, 1883.

HICKEY, JOHN, *Irregularities and Simple Impediments*, Washington, 1920.

HICKEY, J. S., *Summula Philosophiae Scholasticae*, 5 ed., 3 vols., Dublinii, 1919.

HILARIUS A SEXTEN, *Tractatus de Censuris Ecclesiasticis*, Moguntiae, 1898.

HINSCHIUS, P., *System des Katholischen Kirchenrechts*, vol. 4, Berlin, 1888.

HOLWECK, JOS., *Die Kirchliche Strafgazetze*, Mainz, 1899. 1899.

KEARNEY, RICHARD, *Sponsors at Baptism*, Washington, 1925.

KELLEY, JAMES, *The Jurisdiction of the Simple Confessor*, Washington, 1927.

KONINGS, A., *Theologia Moralis*, 3 ed., 2 vols., New York, 1877.

KONINGS-PUTZER, *Commentarium in Facultates Apostolicas*, 3 ed., Ilchestriae, 1893.

LEGA, MICHAEL, *Praelectiones in Textum Juris Canonici de Judiciis Ecclesiasticis*, lib. II, vol. III, Romae, 1899.

LEHMKUHL, AUGUSTINUS, *Theologia Moralis*, 5 ed., 2 vols., Friburgi Brisgoviae, 1884; 12 ed., 2 vols., Friburgi Brisgoviae, 1914.

LEITNER, MARTIN, *Lehrbuch des katholischen Eherechts*, 3 ed., Paderborn, 1920.

LIGOURI, S. ALPHONSUS, *Theologia Moralis*, 10 vols., Mechliniae, 1842-1845.

LINNEBORN, JOANNES, *Grundriss des Eherechts nach dem Codex Juris Canonici*, 2 & 3 ed., Paderborn, 1922.

MACEVILLY, *An Exposition of the Epistles of Saint Paul*, etc., Vol. I, Dublin, 1875.

————————, *An Exposition of the Gospels (Matthew and Mark)*, 3 ed., New York, 1888.

MAROTO, PHILIPPUS, *Institutiones Juris Canonici ad Normam Novi Codicis*, 2 vols., Madrid, 1919.

MARTIN, MICHAEL, *The Roman Curia*, New York, 1913.

MAZZELLA, CAMILLUS, *De Religione et Ecclesia*, 4 ed., Romae, 1892.

MIGNE, *Patrologia Graeca*, 161 vols., Parisiis, 1857-1866.

————————, *Patrologia Latina*, 221 vols., Parisiis, 1844-1855.

MOTRY, HUBERT, *Diocesan Faculties according to the Code of Canon Law*, Washington, 1922.

MURPHY, GEORGE, *Delinquencies and Penalties in the Administration and Reception of the Sacraments,* Washington, 1923.

MURRAY, PATRICK, *Tractatus De Ecclesia Christi,* Dublinii, 1860.

NAVARRUS, MARTINUS, *Opera Omnia,* 6 vols., Venetiis, 1618-1621.

NOLDIN, H., *Summa Theologiae Moralis,* vol. I, 17 ed.; vol. II, 16 ed.; vol. III, 15 & 16 ed., Oeniponte, 1923-1924.

NOLDIN-SCHÖNEGGER, *De Censuris,* 14 & 15 ed., Oeniponte, 1923.

NOVAL, JOSEPHUS, *De Processibus,* pars I, *De Judiciis,* Augustae Taurinorum, 1920.

O'KEEFFE, GERALD, *Matrimonial Dispensations, Powers of Bishops, Priests, and Confessors,* Washington, 1927.

PASCHANG, JOHN, *The Sacramentals,* Washington, 1925.

PERRONE, JOANNES, *Praelectiones Theologiae,* 8 vols., Romae, 1840-1844.

PESCH, CHRISTIANUS, *Praelectiones Dogmaticae,* 9 vols., Friburgi Brisgoviae, 1898.

PETROVITS, JOSEPH, *The New Church Law on Matrimony,* Philadelphia, 1921; 2 ed., Philadelphia, 1926.

PIGHI, J. B., *Censurae Sententiae Latae et Irregularitates quas habet Codex Juris Canonici,* Veronae, 1922.

PRUEMMER, DOMINICUS, *Manuale Juris Canonici,* 3 ed., Friburgi Brisgoviae, 1922.

——————, *Manuale Theologiae Moralis,* 2 & 3 ed., 3 vols., Friburgi Brisgoviae, 1923.

QUIGLEY, JOSEPH, *Condemned Societies,* Washington, 1927.

REIFFENSTUEL, ANACLETUS, *Jus Canonicum Universum,* 4 vols., Venetiis, 1735.

ROBERTI, FRANCISUS, *De Processibus,* vol. I, Romae, 1926.

SABETTI, ALOYSIUS, *Compendium Theologiae Moralis,* 3 ed., Neo Eboraci, 1888.

SALMANTICENSES, *Cursus Theologiae Moralis,* Venetiis, 1714.

SALUCCI, RAFFAELE, *Il Diritto Penale secondo il Codice di Diritto Canonico,* vol. I, Subiaco, 1926.

SCHMALZGRUEBER, FRANCISCUS, *Jus Ecclesiasticum Universum,* 12 vols., Romae, 1843-1845.

SCHMIDT, ANTONIUS, *Thesaurus Juris Ecclesiastici Potissimum Germanici,* Heidelbergae, 1779.

SEISENBERGER, MICHAEL, *Practical Handbook for the Study of the Bible and of Bible Literature,* translated from 6 German edition by A. M. Buchanan, New York, 1911.

SELDEN, JOANNES, *Opera Omnia,* 3 vols., Londini, 1726.

SMITH, S. B., *Elements of Ecclesiastical Law,* vol. III, *Ecclesiastical Punishments,* 3 ed., New York, 1888.

SMITH, WILLIAM, *Dictionary of Bible,* revised and edited by Hackett and Abbot, 4 vols., New York, 1869.

SOLE, JACOBUS, *De Delictis et Poenis,* Romae, 1920.

SUAREZ, FRANCISCUS, *Opera Omnia,* 26 vols., Parisiis, 1861.

TACITUS, *Germania.*

TANQUEREY, AD., *Synopsis Theologiae Dogmaticae,* 19 ed., Romae, 1922.

VECCHIOTTI, S., *Institutiones Canonicae ex operibus Joannis Card. Soglia excerptae,* 16 ed., 3 vols., Augustae Taurinorum, 1875.

VERMEERSCH-CREUSEN, *Epitome Juris Canonici,* 2 ed., 3 vols., Mechliniae, 1924-1925.

VIGOUROUX, F., *Dictionnaire de la Bible,* 5 vols., Paris, 1895-1912.

VLAMING, TH. M., *Praelectiones Juris Matrimonii ad Normam Codicis Juris Canonici,* 3 ed., 2 vols., Bussum in Hollandia, 1919-1921.

WERNZ, FRANCISCUS, *Jus Decretalium,* 3 ed., 8 vols., Prati, 1913.

WERNZ-VIDAL, *Jus Canonicum,* vols. II, V, VI, Romae, 1923-1925.

WOYWOD, STANISLAUS, *The New Canon Law. A Commentary and Summary of the New Code of Canon Law,* 3 ed., New York, 1918. (This work has been used as a guide in translating the canons.)

WOYWOD, STANISLAUS, *A Practical Commentary on the New Code of Canon Law,* 2 vols., New York, 1925-1926.

ABBREVIATIONS

AAS—Acta Apostolicae Sedis.

ASS—Acta Sanctae Sedis.

Coll. S. C. P. F.—Collectanea S. Congregationis de Propaganda Fide.

Fontes—Codicis Juris Canonici Fontes.

MPG—MIGNE, J. P., *Patrologiae Cursus Completus—Series Graeca.*

MPL—MIGNE, J. P., *Patrologiae Cursus Completus—Series Latina.*

S. C. S. Off.—Sacra Congregatio Sancti Officii.

Universitas Catholica America

Washingtonii, D. C.

Facultas Juris Canonici

1927-1928

No. 49

DEUS LUX MEA

THESES

QUAS

AD DOCTORATUS GRADUM

IN

JURE CANONICO

Apud Universitatem Catholicam Americae

CONSEQUENDUM

PUBLICE PROPUGNABIT

FRANCISCUS EDUARDUS HYLAND

SACERDOS ARCHIDIOECESIS

PHILADELPHIENSIS

JURIS CANONICI LICENTIATUS

HORA XI A. M. DIE I JUNII A. D. MCMXXVIII

I. De Relatione inter Ecclesiam et Statum.
II. De Dissertatione.
III. De Historia Juris Canonici.
IV. Canones 1-7, De Ambitu Codicis.
V. Canones 8-24, De Legibus Ecclesiasticis.
VI. Canones 25-30, De Consuetudine.
VII. Canones 31-35, De Temporis Supputatione.
VIII. Canones 36-63, De Rescriptis.
IX. Canones 63-79, De Privilegiis.
X. Canones 80-86, De Dispensatione.
XI. Canones 356-362, De Synodo Dioecesana.
XII. Canones 363-390, De Curia Dioecesana.
XIII. Canones 423-428, De Consultoribus Dioecesanis.
XIV. Canones 451-478, De Parochis et Vicariis Paroecialibus.
XV. Canones 479-486, De Ecclesiarum Rectoribus.
XVI. Canones 726-730, De Simonia.
XVII. Canones 951-991, De Ministro et Subjecto Sacrae Ordinationis.
XVIII. Canones 1019-1034, De iis quae Matrimonii Celebrationi praemitti debent.
XIX. Canones 1035-1080, De Impedimentis Matrimonialibus.
XX. Canones 1081-1093, De Consensu Matrimoniali.
XXI. Canones 1094-1107, De Forma Celebrationis Matrimonii.
XXII. Canones 1108-1109, De Tempore et Loco Celebrationis Matrimonii.
XXIII. Canones 1110-1117, De Matrimonii Effectibus.
XXIV. Canones 1118-1132, De Separatione Conjugum.
XXV. Canones 1133-1141, De Matrimonii Convalidatione.

XXVI. Canones 1556-1568, De Foro Competenti.

XXVII. Canones 1572-1593, De Tribunali Ordinario Primae Instantiae.

XXVIII. Canones 1594-1596, De Tribunali Ordinario Secundae Instantiae.

XXIX. Canones 1597-1605, De Ordinariis Apostolicae Sedis Tribunalibus.

XXX. Canones 1608-1626, De Officio Judicum et Tribunalis Ministrorum.

XXXI. Canones 1627-1633, De Ordine Cognitionum.

XXXII. Canones 1640-1645, De Personis ad Disceptationem Judicialem Admittendis et de Modo Confectionis et Conservationis Actorum.

XXXIII. Canones 1646-1666, De Partibus in Causa.

XXXIV. Canones 1667-1705, De Actionibus et Exceptionibus.

XXXV. Canones 1706-1725, De Causae Introductione.

XXXVI. Canones 1726-1731, De Litis Contestatione.

XXXVII. Canones 1732-1741, De Litis Instantia.

XXXVIII. Canones 1742-1746, De Interrogationibus Partibus in Judicio Faciendis.

XXXIX. Canones 1747-1769, De Probationibus.

XL. Canones 1960-1992, De Causis Matrimonialibus.

XLI. Canones 1993-1998, De Causis contra Sacram Ordinationem.

XLII. Canones 2147-2167, De Remotione et Translatione Parochorum.

XLIII. Canones 2168-2185, De Modo Procedendi contra Clericos non Residentes, etc.

XLIV. Canones 2186-2194, De Modo Procedendi in Suspensione ex Informata Conscientia Infligenda.

XLV. Canones 2214-2254, De Poenis et Censuris in Genere.

Roman Law

XLVI. Periods of Roman Law.
XLVII. Personality.
XLVIII. Citizenship.
XLIX. The Roman Family.
L. *Cura* and *Tutela.*
LI. Adoption.
LII. Roman Marriage.
LIII. Modes of Acquiring Singular Things.
LIV. Modes of Acquiring an Aggregate of Things.
LV. General Character of Obligation.
LVI. Classification of Obligations.
LVII. General Principles of Contracts.
LVIII. Real Contracts.
LIX. Verbal Contracts.
LX. Literal Contracts.

VIDIT FACULTAS:

PHILIPPUS BERNARDINI, S. T. D., J. U. D., Decanus.

LUDOVICUS MOTRY, S. T. D., J. C. D., a Secretis.

VALENTINUS SCHAAF, O. F. M., J. C. D.
FRANCISCUS LARDONE, S. T. D., J. U. D.

VIDIT RECTOR UNIVERSITATIS:
† THOMAS J. SHAHAN, S. T. D., J. U. L., LL.D.

BIOGRAPHICAL NOTE

Francis Edward Hyland was born in Philadelphia, Penna., on October 9, 1901. He made his primary and secondary studies in the parochial schools and in the Roman Catholic High School of Philadelphia. In September, 1918, he entered St. Charles Seminary, Overbrook, Penna. In the fall of 1926, he began graduate studies in the School of Canon Law at the Catholic University. He was ordained to the Holy Priesthood in June, 1927. In the same month, the degrees of Bachelor and Licentiate in Canon Law were conferred upon him. In partial fulfilment of the requirements for the Doctorate in Canon Law, he wrote and published this dissertation on the Censure of Excommunication.

www.ingramcontent.com/pod-product-compliance
Lightning Source LLC
LaVergne TN
LVHW050233080826
844660LV00012B/524

* 9 7 8 0 8 1 3 2 2 2 3 8 7 *